Blood Money

A thriller

The Heather Brothers

Samuel French — London
New York - Toronto - Hollywood

BLOOD MONEY

First presented at the Derby Playhouse on 6th May 1994
with the following cast:

Mike Mason	Ben Roberts
Sue Thompson	Emily Joyce
Elizabeth Mason	Eliza McClelland
Dr Campbell	Sally Faulkner

Director Mark Clements
Designer Chris Crosswell
Lighting designer Chris Ellis
Musical underscore David Roper

Subsequently produced by Bernard Havard in an American
version at the Walnut Street Theatre, Philadelphia, on
23rd September 1995 with the following cast:

Mike Mason	Alan Feinstein
Sue Thompson	Juliette Dunn
Elizabeth Mason	Kathleen Doyle
Dr Campbell	Patricia Hodges
Awards Show Host	Nancy Glass

Director Mark Clements
Designer Chris Crosswell
Lighting designer Chris Ellis
Musical underscore David Roper

CHARACTERS

Mike Mason
Sue Thompson
Elizabeth Mason
Dr Julie Campbell

Voices only:
Carol Mitchell
Policewoman
Policeman

The action takes place in the lounge of the Masons' home, Sussex, England and at a Television Awards ceremony*

Time — the present

SYNOPSIS OF SCENES

* *American Version* — The Masons' home is in New Hope, Pennsylvania, and the ceremony is for the Emmy Awards
See pp. 70-72 for an English/American glossary

Other plays by the Heather Brothers
published by Samuel French Ltd:

Lust
A Slice of Saturday Night

ACT I
SCENE 1

The lounge of the Masons' home. Winter. 5.30 p.m.

The lounge is a large room in a handsomely converted barn. A heavy oak door, complete with ornate wrought-iron hinges, ringed door handle and upper and lower bolts, leads to an enclosed porch and unseen front door. A second door leads to the kitchen. Curtains and interior wooden shutters protect the double-glazed french windows which open out on to a shrubbery-flanked patio. A stairway, with a cupboard under it, leads to the upper floor. Against a wall, between the stairs and the porch door, stands an ornate 1950s' juke-box in pristine condition. Above it hangs a tapestry. The rest of the furniture includes a sofa, an old rocking chair, drinks cabinet, a desk with a lap-top computer and papers on it, bookcases loaded with books, a coffee table with two glasses on it, a television and video, various occasional tables and a telephone. There is also a wall safe. A decorative china plate hangs from one wall and there are various ornaments on shelves and tables. The room has a number of concealed domestic spotlights and table lamps, enabling various areas to be lit while leaving the rest of the room in shadow

When the play begins there is a light coming from the juke-box and the wall safe is open. The curtains are closed and moonlight shines through them from outside

As the house lights go down, there is a sudden loud music chord

After a moment, the figure of a man — Mike Mason, in fact, though he cannot at first be recognized in the darkness — emerges from the shadows and moves stealthily towards the stairs. He is in his forties and has the smooth good looks of the ladies' man he certainly considers himself to be. He is wearing a black polo neck with a white dress shirt beneath it and evening dress trousers and is carrying a gun and torch which we do not see as yet. He bumps into something; there is a clatter. He freezes, then quickly moves to the shadows at the foot of the stairs

A door opens at the head of the stairs and light spills on to the landing

Sue Thompson enters and looks nervously down. She is an attractive twenty-year-old, wearing a dress and jumper

Sue (*frightened*) Who's there?

Silence

(*Edging down the stairs*) Look, I know there's someone down there.

Sue is half-way down the stairs when Mike steps out of the shadows and shines a torch in her face. He points the gun at her

Mike Come here.

Sue, blinded by the light, is transfixed with fear

Sue (*terrified*) Oh my God ... who are you?
Mike I said, "Come here".
Sue (*coming down the stairs, terrified*) What are you going to do ... ? Oh my God, what are you going to do? (*She reaches the foot of the stairs and moves to Mike, still blinded by the torch light*)
Mike (*indicating Sue's jumper with the gun*) Take it off.
Sue What?
Mike (*viciously*) Take it off!

Sue takes off her jumper

(*As she does this*) I've been watching you all evening ... all evening.

Sue drops the jumper on to the floor

Now that dress.
Sue Please — don't hurt me.
Mike Just do it!

Whimpering, Sue unbuttons the front of her dress and lets it drop to the floor; she is wearing a slip underneath

The phone rings

Sue Oh, God.
Mike Oh, shit! Perfect timing.

Sue steps up to Mike, puts her arms round his neck and starts kissing him

Sue Leave it.

The telephone continues to ring

Mike (*annoyed*) It's no good. I'm sorry, I'm going to have to answer it. Stay exactly where you are, we'll pick up where we left off.
Sue You and your little games.

Mike switches on the table lamp by the sofa

Mike (*answering the phone*) Hallo, the Masons' residence.

Julie's voice is heard over a speaker, as if coming from the phone

Julie (*from the phone*) Michael, it's Julie.
Mike Oh hi, how are you? (*He covers the mouthpiece; to Sue*) It's my agent.
Julie (*from the phone*) All set for tonight?
Mike Absolutely.
Julie (*from the phone*) How are you feeling?
Mike Couldn't be better.
Julie (*from the phone*) You are?
Mike Yeah, really, I'm fine.
Julie (*from the phone*) You sound a bit tense.
Mike Well under the circumstances ——

Sue tickles Mike

   (*Breaking off*) — aah!
Julie (*from the phone*) I beg your pardon?
Mike Nothing ... nothing ... I — er ...

Sue tickles Mike again

   (*Covering the mouthpiece*) Please, this is business.

Pulling a face at him, Sue moves to the juke-box. She stands reading the song titles during the following

Julie (*from the phone*) Michael, are you sure you're all right?
Mike Yes, yes ... honestly, Julie, I'm fine ...

Sue gives Mike a puzzled look, then goes back to reading the titles

   Look, I thought we agreed — you know ...
Julie (*from the phone*) I wouldn't call you at home.

Mike Yeah.

Julie (*from the phone*) I wouldn't have. It's just that ...

Mike What?

Julie (*from the phone*) Michael, you haven't let anything slip, have you?

Mike How do you mean?

Julie (*from the phone*) To Liz ... about us. You haven't said anything?

Mike Course not. Why?

Julie (*from the phone*) Well, it's just that ... (*Hesitantly*) Look, I'm not trying to worry you, but I think Liz may suspect something.

Mike (*looking at Sue; apprehensively*) What makes you think that?

Julie (*from the phone*) Well, I bumped into her at lunchtime at the Country Club ...

Mike And?

Julie (*from the phone*) She was ... I don't know — different.

Mike Did she say anything?

Julie (*from the phone*) Not in so many words. It was her attitude. I just got the feeling she knew something ... How is she at home?

Mike (*glancing at Sue*) Same as usual .... You're sure you're not imagining this?

Julie (*from the phone*) I don't know, maybe I am. Maybe I'm reading more into it than there is.

Mike You're not having second thoughts are you, Julie? You're positive you want to go through with this?

Julie (*from the phone*) Of course I am. We've no other choice, Michael. Things can't carry on as they are.

Mike You don't have to convince me.

Julie (*from the phone*) If we want a future together, we have to do something.

Mike My sentiments exactly. As far as I'm concerned, the sooner I'm out of it, the better. (*He puts his hand over the mouthpiece; to Sue*) Damn contracts.

Julie (*from the phone*) I'm sorry I phoned you at home. It's probably just my imagination ——

A car is heard driving up. Headlights sweep the drive

Sue (*peering through the windows, surprised*) A taxi's just pulled up.

Julie (*from the phone*) — but I thought I'd better warn you just in case.

Mike (*covering the mouthpiece, to Sue*) A taxi?

Sue Oh, my God! It's your wife!

During the following, Sue frantically gets dressed

Mike (*alarmed*) I've got to go, Julie, Liz has showed up.

Julie (*from the phone*) But she's supposed to be at the Clinic.
Mike (*hanging up*) I've got to go.

In a burst of frenzied activity, Mike pulls off the polo neck to reveal the white dress shirt and rushes around tidying up the room. He puts the gun into the wall safe and closes it. During the following, the porch light comes on

Sue I thought you said she was at the Clinic.
Mike She's supposed to be ... For God's sake, hurry up.
Sue (*looking round desperately*) My jumper ... where the hell did you put my jumper?
Mike (*throwing it at her*) Here.

Mike picks up the glasses from the coffee table and runs into the kitchen

Sue struggles to put her jumper on; it ends up inside out

Mike enters and switches on the main lights

(*Noticing Sue's jumper*) Sue, it's inside out.
Sue Oh, my God!

Sue whips her jumper off and turns it the right way round. Mike signals for Sue to sit in the rocking chair. She dashes across to it and sits. As she does so ——

Elizabeth (Liz) Mason enters. She looks to be in her forties, but is probably younger. Although once glamorous, an over-indulgence in alcohol has taken its toll. She is dressed in expensive casual clothes. It is obvious she has been drinking

Mike and Sue try to appear calm and relaxed

Liz Why, look who's here again. Little Susie Thompson from next door.
Mike (*in mock surprise*) Liz ... ? What are you doing here?
Liz I live here, Mike. Remember?
Mike I thought you were going to the Clinic.
Liz (*looking at them, knowingly*) Of course, I was supposed to be at the Clinic, wasn't I ...? (*As though having a sudden thought*) Oooo — I hope I haven't interrupted anything.
Mike (*trying to make light of it*) I should be so lucky. (*He laughs*) No, no, Sue just popped over to wish me luck. Isn't that sweet of her?
Liz (*insincerely*) Very.

There is an embarrassed silence

Sue You must be very excited, Liz.

Liz Really? About what?

Sue Tonight.

Liz Tonight?

Mike (*wearily*) The awards ceremony, Liz.

Liz Oh, that ... Yes, ecstatic. I can hardly contain myself.

Sue I was just telling Mike, all my friends'll be keeping their fingers crossed for him.

Liz (*insincerely*) Is that right? Isn't that sweet, Mike ... ? Mind you, it'll take more than crossed fingers for you to win, won't it, pet? More like divine intervention.

Mike As you've no doubt gathered, Liz doesn't rate my chances too highly.

Liz Correction, Liz doesn't rate your chances, period ... You see, Sue, to win the "Television Personality of the Year Award", one must have a personality.

Mike (*trying to laugh it off*) Yes, all right, Liz.

Liz Well, it's true, pet. I'd have thought even you would've known that. Either wit, charm, personality — something outstanding ...

Mike To hear Liz, no one'd think I'd been nominated every year for the last seven years.

Liz Yes, but you've never won, have you, pet? (*To Sue*) I keep telling the poor dear, they only nominated him to make up the numbers.

Sue (*laughing, embarrassed*) I'm sure you don't mean that, Liz.

Liz Don't I? Why else would they have nominated him then?

Sue (*flustered*) Well ... after all, Mike is a household name.

Liz So is Armitage Shanks, dear, and they weren't — (*to Mike*) even though they deal in the same commodity ... (*To Sue*) Personally, I don't think they should be allowed to broadcast rubbish like "Bargain Basement" without a government health warning.

Mike As you so delight in telling everyone.

Liz Well, I may be a lot of things, Mike, but a hypocrite I am not. If I don't like something, I say so, even if it does mean denting your ego. (*To Sue*) They actually have the gall to advertise it as "light entertainment"; I'm surprised they haven't been prosecuted under the Trades Descriptions Act. (*To Mike*) Entertainment — it's nothing but mindless drivel. (*To Sue*) Don't you agree, Sue?

Sue (*embarrassed*) Well, no ... I wouldn't describe it as mindless drivel.

Liz Oh? So how would you describe "Mike Mason's Bargain Basement"? Intellectually stimulating?

Sue No, of course not.

Liz How about intellectually mindless stimulating drivel?

Mike (*pleasantly*) Let's just drop it, shall we, Liz?

Liz (*innocently*) What's wrong, Mike? Aren't we interested in what the "younger" generation think of your show?

Mike It's not supposed to be *Open University*. It's a game show, love. Just a little bit of fun, that's all.

Liz Really? A little bit of fun? (*To Sue*) I'd never have guessed.

Sue Actually, I think it's great.

Liz There's no need to be polite on Mike's account, dear.

Sue I'm not being polite. I really do enjoy it.

Liz (*suggestively*) I'm sure you do. (*She looks at Mike*) But then, I suppose there's no accounting for taste ... Can I get you a drink?

Sue No thanks, Mike's already given me one.

Liz Really? (*To Mike*) I thought you said I hadn't interrupted anything.

Mike (*embarrassed*) Liz ...

Liz (*with mock innocence*) It was a joke, love ... You're not offended are you, Sue?

Sue No, of course not.

Liz (*moving to the drinks. To Mike*) There you are, what did I tell you? (*To Sue*) He's such an old stuffed shirt. (*She pours herself a drink during the following*)

Sue What always amazes me, Mike, is how you manage to think of those ad-libs.

Liz (*laughs*) Good God, you don't actually think he makes them up, do you, Sue? He reads them off those card thingies. Don't you, Mike?

Mike Some of it's scripted, yes.

Liz Some of it ... ? (*To Sue*) It's a standing joke with the crew that Mike wouldn't remember his own name if it wasn't written up on one of those ... what do you call them again? Oh yes. Idiot cards.

The phone rings

Liz picks up the phone

(*Into phone*) Hallo, Mike Mason's House of Ill-repute.

No answer; there is silence on the other end of the telephone

Hallo ... ? Hallo ... ?

The caller hangs up; the dialling tone is heard

Strange. That's the fourth time it's happened this week.

Mike What is?

Liz (*replacing the receiver*) Someone's hung up on me.

Mike Probably a wrong number.

Liz Either that or it wasn't me they wanted to talk to.

Mike Meaning?

Liz Meaning it's peculiar how it only happens when *I* answer the phone.

Mike In other words, you think it was for me. Is that what you're saying?

Liz I just find it rather odd, that's all. (*To Sue*) Of course, if I had a suspicious nature, I might think there was something going on behind my back.

Mike Don't be ridiculous.

Sue Actually, I really should be going.

Mike There's nothing going on behind your back.

Liz Nobody said there was, pet. I was simply pointing out that if I did have a suspicious nature, it could conceivably look that way. (*To Sue*) Mind you, if he was fooling around behind my back, he'd hardly tell me, would he, Sue? (*To Mike*) At least you never have in the past.

Mike Liz, let's talk about this later, all right ... ?

Liz (*interrupting*) You know, I really would appreciate it, Mike, if you didn't give your "lady friends" our home number ——

Mike (*to himself*) Here we go.

Liz (*to Sue*) — I don't think that's too much to ask, do you? I really don't see why I should be subjected to this sort of thing.

Mike Liz, I don't know what you're talking about.

Sue I really should leave ...

Liz No, no, no, of course you don't, pet. I'm being totally unreasonable as usual, aren't I?

Mike I didn't say that.

Liz But that's what you're implying. (*To Sue*) What do you think, Sue?

Mike Leave Sue out of this.

Liz (*innocently*) I'm just asking a question. (*To Sue*) Sue, do you think I'm being unreasonable? If every time you answered the phone someone hung up, wouldn't you find it just a teensie-weensie bit suspicious?

Sue (*embarrassed*) Look, I'm sorry, Liz, but I really don't think this has anything to do with me.

Mike Exactly. Now let's drop it, shall we? (*To Sue*) I'm sorry about this.

Liz (*turning on him, furious*) What did you say?

Mike What ... ?

Liz Just then. To Sue. What did you say?

Mike Liz ...

Liz (*to Sue*) He apologized for me, didn't he? (*To Mike*) How dare you! If anyone deserves an apology, it's me!

Mike (*calm*) Liz, you're making a fool of yourself.

Liz That's right! Go on, twist it round, Mike. You're very good at that, aren't you. Twisting things around. Making it appear I'm in the wrong. Nothing's

ever your fault, is it? Oh no, never good old Mike's. It's always Liz. Liz
over-reacting. Liz being unreasonable. Liz making a fool of herself. It's
always Liz, isn't it, Mike? Always me. Always my fault.

There is an embarrassed silence

Sue (*checking her wrist-watch*) Right, well, I'll be off then. Thanks for the
drink.
Mike I'll show you out. Thanks for coming over.
Sue My pleasure. It's all right, I'll see myself out.
Mike You'll do no such thing.
Sue Bye, Liz.
Liz Ciao.

Mike and Sue exit through the porch

Sue (*off*) Good luck for tonight.
Mike (*off*) Thanks. Bye.

The front door is heard closing

Mike enters

Where the hell have you been?
Liz Out.
Mike I realize that.
Liz Then why ask.
Mike (*furiously*) You've been drinking, haven't you?
Liz I refuse to answer on the grounds I'll never hear the end of it.
Mike You were at the club drinking. Don't lie. Someone saw you.
Liz All right, all right, I confess, I stopped at the club for one teensie-weensie
drinkie.
Mike One? Since when did they start serving vodka by the bucket?
Liz (*unconcerned*) So I had a couple. I know my girlish figure belies the fact,
but I am over eighteen, Mike. (*She stumbles, then steadies herself*)
Mike Look at you. You can't even stand.
Liz Not true. If I couldn't stand, I wouldn't be able to fall over. (*She falls
backwards on to the sofa, giggling*)
Mike You know how important tonight is, how much it means to me.
Couldn't you have restrained yourself just this once?
Liz Obviously not.
Mike Well, thank you very much.
Liz (*smiling sweetly*) Any time.

Mike What's the point in spending a goddamn fortune on a therapist to sort out your drink problem if instead of going to the Clinic you go and get smashed? Not only is it a waste of everybody's time, it's a complete waste of goddamn money. Do you know what I think?

Liz I'm not in the least bit interested in what you think, Mike.

Mike You're not interested in anything unless it comes out of a bottle. I think you went out and got smashed just to piss me off.

Liz Don't flatter yourself. I can assure you, pet, my motives were completely selfish. I had to anaesthetize myself against tonight's barrage of self-congratulatory schmaltz ... Anyway, what's the big deal? No one's going to notice. Everyone's drunk at these "do"s.

Mike By the time they leave, dear, not when they arrive.

Liz Yeah? Well, you should count yourself lucky I've agreed to go. I can assure you I've better ways to spend an evening than watching you chat up every cute-arsed bimbo that wanders within striking distance.

Mike So why are you coming? Nobody forced you.

Liz Matrimonial duty, my darling. A wife's place is at a husband's side at moments of great disappointment.

Mike Screw you!

Liz (*sweetly*) Oooooh, language, Mike.

There is a pause

Mike Look, it's obvious you don't want to go. Why not do us both a favour and stay at home?

Liz Oh, but I couldn't do that, Mike. Like I said, my place is at your side — cramping your style.

Mike Oh, I see, it's going to be one of those evenings, again, is it?

Liz Looks like it.

Mike (*weary*) Suit yourself. But if you are coming, go and get changed. I thought we'd try and arrive on time for once. If that's all right with you?

Liz (*rising to her feet*) For you, pet, anything. (*She moves to Mike; turning her back*) Could you?

Mike undoes Liz's necklace. She turns and puts her arms round Mike

(*Nuzzling his neck. Amorous*) Mmmmmmm.

Mike Liz ...

Liz starts kissing his neck

Liz What's wrong? The old clutch starting to slip? The old Jack-in-the-box gone on strike?

Mike You're pathetic.

Liz Something tells me I've touched a raw nerve.

Mike You touch a raw nerve every time you open your mouth.

Liz Or could it be we're still recovering from this evening's exertions with "Sweet Sultry Sue"?

Mike Oh, I give up.

Liz Don't play the innocent with me, Mike. I know what you two were up to.

Mike She came over to wish me luck.

Liz Oh, I see ... and one good turn deserves another.

Mike Liz ——

Liz (*interrupting*) Don't bother lying, for God's sake. It was perfectly obvious what she was here for, prancing round dressed like that ... credit me with some intelligence, please.

Mike Dressed like what? What's she supposed to wear? Overalls?

Liz starts climbing the stairs

Liz, nothing's been going on.

Liz ignores him

I don't know what the hell's wrong with you these days. I only have to talk to a woman and you have me in bed with her.

Liz (*turning on Mike, furiously*) You can screw whoever you want for all I care, but not in this house. Understand? Do I make myself clear? This is my home. Don't you ever bring your women back here again.

Mike Liz, I'm old enough to be the girl's father.

Liz (*cold*) Knowing you, pet, you probably are.

Liz exits

Mike (*calling after her*) Look, if I wanted to fool around with Sue Thompson, I'd hardly bring her back here, would I? I'm not that stupid.

There is no answer

OK, fine, believe what you want. I can't be bothered arguing any more ... Damn woman.

Mike starts to put his tie on

(*Reciting to himself*) "Ladies and Gentlemen. What can I say, I'm speechless, absolutely speechless — no, no, literally speechless — I was so certain I didn't stand a chance, I didn't bother writing one. Writing one ... " (*He forgets his words*) Oh shit! (*He takes a piece of paper from his pocket and reads from it*) "Now I know it's usual —— "

Liz (*off, sweetly*) Mike ...

Mike " — I know it's usual on these occasions for the guy who wins to bore the pants off all and sundry thanking everyone they feel is instrumental in them winning ... "

Liz (*off, calling, sweetly*) Mike ...

Mike Yeah, what is it?

Liz Which dress would you like me to wear? The peach one or the yellow one?

Mike I don't know — suit yourself.

Liz How about the red?

Mike No! Definitely not the red.

Liz Which then, the yellow or the peach?

Mike The yellow one.

Liz (*incredulous*) You want me to wear the yellow one?

Mike (*weary*) Yes.

Liz Are you absolutely positive?

Mike (*irritated*) Yes.

Liz All right, darling, after all, it's your night.

Mike (*finding his place in the speech*) "... instrumental in his winning ... don't get me wrong, I'm not knocking it. No, no, credit where credit's due, I mean, it's only right: if someone helps you, thank them. However, saying that, tonight I'm breaking with that tradition. I'm not going to name a single name. Not one ...

He exits into the kitchen

(*Off*) Ungrateful pillock, that's what you're thinking — right? Wrong? Couldn't be further from the truth. I'm not naming names, not because I don't want to, but because it's just not humanly possible. You see, the people responsible for me standing here tonight ——

He enters, carrying a cup of coffee

— the proud winner of this prestigious award, are you, the great British public, who by faithfully tuning in week after week have made "Mike Mason's Bargain Basement" this nation's undisputed number one game show. "Going, going, gone!" And so to each and every one of you out there tonight, I'd like to take this opportunity to say ——

Liz appears in a red dress, carrying a handbag

(*Seeing Liz*) Thank you very much."

Liz I thought you'd appreciate it.

Mike It's about par for the course these days, isn't it? (*He points to the coffee*) Here, drink this.

Liz (*with mock horror*) Coffee ... ? Good God, you're not trying to sober me up, are you?

Mike (*wearily*) Just drink it.

Liz (*brightly*) Any chance of lacing it with a drop of brandy? No, I thought not.

Mike We'll be sitting with the Cochranes this evening, so don't do anything embarrassing, all right?

Liz Embarrassing ... ? Oh, you mean like attempting to engage the poor dears in an intelligent conversation?

Mike No, like acting frigging superior.

Liz It's so difficult not to with the Cochranes. They're such incredible philistines. Then again, I suppose being a philistine is an essential quality for someone producing a moronic load of crap like "Bargain Basement" — or presenting it for that matter. (*She impersonates Mike*) "Evening, Ladies and Gentlemen, this is 'Mike Mason's Bargain Basement', where everything goes ... (*suggestively*) ... for a price! So girls, if you're looking for that special something, remember, you'll find it in Mike's — two pelvic thrusts — Basement. Going, going, gone ... "

Mike (*angrily*) You're so full of shit, you know that? What did you ever do? Hey? A goddamn actress who made a career out of auditions. I know gratitude was never your strong point, Liz, but you want to remember if it wasn't for those philistines and that "moronic load of crap", as you so eloquently put it, I'd still be scratching a living working the clubs and we, my darling, would still be living in some grotty bedsit above a newsagent's.

Liz (*calm*) There's no need to raise your voice, Mike. If you've got something to say, say it. You don't have to shout.

Mike It's the only way to penetrate that vodka-sodden sponge you call a brain. The Cochranes may lack your acquired social graces, dear heart, but as long as they pay my salary, and you're prepared to spend it, you'll treat them with respect. Do I make myself clear? I couldn't care less if you think they're the biggest bunch of assholes you've ever met, tonight you'll be polite, you will be gracious, you will radiate warmth and charm. Got it? Good! Now drink that coffee and get yourself sober! After all, we wouldn't want you throwing up all over the Waldorf, now would we?

Liz (*thoughtfully*) A vein in your forehead starts throbbing when you get excited, Mike. I never noticed it before. Throb, throb, throb ... Sorry, you were saying?

Mike Oh, I've had it with you.

Liz Not for the last six months you haven't — unless I was reading and didn't notice.

Mike Typical. Snide remarks, accusations, arguments, day in, day out. Well,
   I've had enough. Tomorrow I'm getting the hell out of here.

Liz How many times have I heard that?

Mike Yeah? Well, this time I mean it.

Liz You always do.

Mike What's the point? We can't stand the sight of each other. We can't hold
   a conversation any more without you turning it into an argument. I mean,
   look at us. We spend our entire time picking holes in one another. Scoring
   points. Well, I'm sorry, but I'm not prepared to put up with it any longer.
   Life's too short.

Liz Leave me and you'll regret it.

Pause

   I mean it, Mike. Leave me and you'll regret it.

For a moment they look at each other. Mike moves up the stairs

   And for your information, Mike, I did not make a career out of auditions.
   You seem to have forgotten I had to turn down work because of you.

Mike You what?

Liz Turned down work. Because your agent, Harry-goddamn-Edison, was
   concerned it might damage your "family image".

Mike (*derisively*) Yeah, right. All topless.

Liz Once.

Mike Once?

Liz Yes, once! And it was an integral part of the plot.

Mike Oh yeah, sure it was.

   Mike exits

Liz (*calling after him*) Well, it was. (*Under her breath*) Bastard. (*She opens
   her handbag and takes out a small pill bottle. Popping a couple in her
   mouth, she takes out a hip flask and washes them down with a long swig*)

The telephone rings

   (*Answering the phone*) Hallo, the Masons' residence.

Breathing is heard from the telephone

   Hallo?

The breathing continues

Hallo ... ? Look, I know someone's there. Whoever you are, will you please stop this nonsense? I'm getting heartily sick of it. Look, this is getting beyond a joke.

From the telephone, a woman is heard crying

(*Confused*) Who is this?

Voice (*from phone, whispered, sobbing*) Help me. Please ... Please help me ——

Liz What's going on?

Voice No, don't ... Don't leave ——

Liz Look, who is this?

The sound of sobbing is heard

Do you want to speak to my husband?

Voice Oh, God, please ... Please don't leave ...

Liz If you don't tell me who you are, I'm going to hang up.

The sobbing continues

(*Angry*) Look, for God's sake, who are you?

The sobbing dies away

Voice Carol Mitchell.

Liz (*stunned*) Who did you say ... ? Who did you say?

The line goes dead

Hallo ... ? Hallo ... ? (*She stands, stunned, holding the telephone; to herself*) Oh, dear God ... (*She replaces the receiver*)

Mike comes down the stairs. He is wearing an evening suit

Mike Are you coming or what?

Liz (*shocked, almost to herself*) Somebody knows — Mike, somebody knows.

Mike About what?

Liz Somebody knows.

Mike What are you talking about?

Liz It's all going to come out, Mike. What are we going to do? Oh, God, what are we going to do?

Mike What the hell's got into you? What's going on?

Liz A woman phoned.

Mike When?

Liz A moment ago. Just before you came down. She was in a terrible state, sobbing, begging for help ... When I asked her who she was, she said she was Carol Mitchell.

Mike You're sick, you know that?

Liz What are we going to do, Mike?

Mike crosses and locks the french windows

Mike, what are we going to do?

Mike I don't know about you, I'm off to London to try and finally win an award.

Liz But the telephone call ——

Mike Yeah? What about it? (*Scathing*) Oh come on, you don't honestly expect me to believe a woman called and said she was Carol Mitchell, do you?

Liz It happened, Mike.

Mike (*sarcastically*) Just when I happened to be out of the room. Very convenient. And how do you suppose this woman got our telephone number. We're unlisted, remember?

Liz I don't know.

Mike If you want me to believe your pathetic little stories, Liz, you really ought to think them through a bit better ... now come on.

Liz (*desperately*) Mike, it happened ...

Mike Come on.

Liz I wouldn't lie about something like this.

Mike Christ, you never give up, do you? Look, you're not going to ruin my night, understand? Now get in the car.

Liz Mike, please, I know it sounds unbelievable, but it's the truth.

Mike looks at her. He shakes his head

You've got to believe me, Mike. A woman called and said she was Carol Mitchell. I don't know how she got our number but she called. I swear, I'm not making it up.

Pause

Mike All right, even if there was a phone call ——

Liz (*interrupting*) There was!

Mike (*deliberately*) Even if there was a phone call, it certainly wasn't Carol Mitchell.

Liz I realize that ... But it means someone knows about us.

Mike How? How could anyone possibly know? Liz, the only people who know what happened that night are you and me. There's no way anyone can link us to Carol Mitchell. Absolutely no way.

Liz But the phone call ...

Mike It was probably a crossed line.

Liz The woman was sobbing, Mike ... begging for help.

Mike You obviously heard it wrong. Let's face it, it wouldn't be the first time you've been confused.

Liz I know what I heard.

Mike Sure. Same as last month you knew someone was following you.

Liz Mike ...

Mike (*interrupting*) Well, you did. You were absolutely certain. No question about it. Someone was following you.

Liz This is different ...

Mike Like all these affairs I'm supposedly having. Like standing in the Mall, screaming at Mary Chambers, because I gave the poor woman a ride home from the station.

Liz Mike, please ...

Mike Like suddenly the house has got an oppressive feeling about it.

Liz Mike, I know what I heard.

Mike We've been living here for eight years and suddenly you're frightened to be here by yourself. You're cracking up.

Liz This is different!

Mike No, this is not different! This is exactly the same! All that booze you've been pouring down your throat has finally caught up with you. It's befuddled your brain. Well, you can tell your precious Dr Campbell from me, it's about time they started getting results. I don't know what they've been doing down that damn Rehab Centre for the last two years, but whatever it is, it's certainly not working.

Liz That's not true.

Mike They're supposed to be getting you off the stuff. Drying you out. It's a goddamn joke. You're worse now than when you started going.

Liz At least at the Clinic they care about me.

Mike And I don't?

Liz No, you don't!

Mike So who sent you there in the first place, hey?

Liz Only because I embarrassed you in front of your friends. You said so yourself. Not because you were concerned about me ... Well, at least whatever Dr Campbell does is for my sake, and nobody else's.

Mike (*scathing*) Oh yeah, right. Grow up, Liz. To them you're just a name on a cheque. Nothing else. They couldn't care less about you.

Liz That's not true. If it wasn't for Dr Campbell, I wouldn't be here now.

Mike Yeah? I'm sick to death of hearing about Dr Campbell. They've done
nothing for you at that Clinic. Anyway, I heard they're going under, so it
can't be that marvellous, can it? I mean, look at you. Half the time you don't
even know where you are ... Now you've started imagining things.
Brilliant!

Liz I didn't imagine the phone call, Mike.

Mike No?

Liz No!

Mike (*calm*) All right ... all right, I accept you believe that's what you heard,
Liz. But try and think rationally for a moment. If someone knew about
Carol Mitchell why would they wait seven years before doing anything?

Liz I don't know.

Mike Why didn't they go straight to the police?

Liz I don't know.

Mike Course you don't. Because it doesn't make bloody sense, that's why.

Liz Mike, whether it makes sense or not, a woman called and said she was
Carol Mitchell.

Mike OK, fine, that's it. I give up. If you want to believe that nonsense, go
ahead, believe it.

Liz But, Mike ...

Mike Liz, nobody can connect us with Carol Mitchell's death. Nobody. Now
get in the car ... and try and stay off the booze.

Mike switches off the lounge lights and he and Liz exit into the porch

*The porch light is switched off leaving the lounge illuminated only by the
moonlight through the curtains. The front door is heard closing; moments
later the car doors slam. The car drives off*

*As it does so, the telephone starts ringing. It continues ringing as the lights
fade to Black-out*

Scene 2

*Note: This scene — ("The Television Award Ceremony") — This scene can
either be done: (a) as written, i.e. on video; (b) as a voice over; or (c) live in
front of the curtain*

From the darkness, the sounds of music, clapping and cheering can be heard

A large screen comes down c. *On it is the caption "Television Personality of
the Year" and a picture of a statuette*

The picture changes to Nancy Edwards, an attractive woman dressed in evening attire. She is standing behind a lectern. Next to her is a statuette

Nancy Hi, this is Nancy Edwards, welcoming you back live to the "Daytime Television Awards", here at the Waldorf Astoria. And without further ado, let's move straight on to our next category, the "Television Personality of the Year". (*She picks up an envelope*) And this year's nominees are: (*she reads*) the host of LWT's ever popular game show, "Gold Rush" — Wayne Dexter!

Music

The picture changes: Wayne Dexter appears. There is the sound of applause, whistles, etc.

The picture reverts to Nancy Edwards

From Channel Four's hilarious game show "Who Said That?", Miss Yackety-Yack herself — Sheri Logan!

The image changes: Sheri Logan appears. Applause, etc.

The screen reverts to Nancy Edwards

Our third nominee, and host of Meridian's perennial favourite, "Bargain Basement", the housewife's choice — Mike Mason!

The image changes to a picture of Mike Mason. Applause, etc.

The screen reverts to Nancy Edwards

And finally, from the BBC's innovative new show, "Against the Odds": its host and our final nominee, Mr Motor-mouth himself — Eddie DeSilva.

The screen changes to a picture of Eddie DeSilva. Applause, etc.

The screen reverts to Nancy Edwards

And the winner is ... (*She opens the envelope, takes out the card and reads*) ... Eddie DeSilva.

The photo of Eddie DeSilva comes up on the screen. Applause, cheering, whistles, etc.

(*Voice-over*)   With his twice weekly show "Against the Odds" now topping the ratings and with talk of a new Saturday slot in the works, there can be no doubt that Eddie DeSilva's quick wit and sparkling repartee has made him "Television Personality of the Year"!

The music and applause fade

Black-out

SCENE 3

The Masons' living-room. Late that night

The room is a total shambles with chairs upturned, drawers pulled out, books and papers strewn everywhere; clothes, including Mike's dressing-gown, litter the stairs and banister

When the scene begins the room is in darkness except for moonlight through a gap in the curtains and the juke-box is playing "Oh, Carol"

Mike (*from the porch, bitterly*) Eddie-frigging-DeSilva. How could anyone in their right mind vote that asshole "Television Personality of the Year"? It's a farce — a frigging farce. The test card's got more personality than that prat!

Liz (*off*) Poor old Mike, always the bridesmaid and never the bride.

Mike (*off*) Ssssh! (*Worriedly*) What the hell's going on?

Mike cautiously enters the lounge and switches on the subdued wall lights

Liz (*off, anxiously*) What is it, Mike?

Mike Jesus Christ!

Liz enters

Liz Oh, no!

Mike We've been broken into ... Turn that damn thing off.

Liz switches off the juke-box

Look at the place, for Chrissake! Just look at it!

Liz Is anything missing?

Mike How the hell should I know? I don't believe this. (*He moves to the stairs*) Stay here.

Liz What ... ?

Mike Just stay here.

Liz (*whispering*) Mike ...

Mike cautiously ascends the stairs and exits

There is a pause, then a crash

Ahhh!
Liz (*worried*) Mike?

Pause

Mike, are you OK? Mike?
Mike (*from upstairs; off*) It's all right. The cupboard was wedged against the
door.

Liz sits on the sofa and takes one of her pills

Mike enters and comes downstairs

Mike You won't believe what it's like up there. It's been totally trashed. The
bathroom, the bedroom, everything. They've been through the whole
damn house. They've ransacked the place.
Liz (*shocked*) Oh, my God! My jewellery ...

Liz rushes upstairs and exits

Mike (*kicking an overturned chair*) Christ, if I get my hands on the bastards
that did this I'll kill 'em! What kind of mentality'd do something like this?
They're just animals. I mean, if you're going to steal something, steal it.
There is no need to tear the place apart.

Liz enters and comes down the stairs

Liz It's still there. My jewellery hasn't been touched. (*She checks the room
during the following*)
Mike Yeah! Well at least the insurance company'll be happy. (*Looking
around*) Where's the phone? Don't tell me that's been stolen. I don't
believe this. (*He finds the phone*) The perfect end to a God-awful evening.
Liz (*confused*) The TV and video are still here.
Mike (*dialling*) So what do you want me to do? Send them a "thank you"
letter?
Liz The safe hasn't been touched, Mike. There's something weird going on.
Nothing seems to have been taken.

Policewoman (*from the telephone*) Burgess Hill Police Station. Can I help
   you?
Mike (*into the telephone*) Er — yes, I'd like to report a break-in at my home.
Policewoman (*from the phone*) Can I have your name and address, please?
Mike Yes, it's Mason ... Mike Mason, 120 Woodbridge Drive.
Policewoman (*from the phone*) Not *the* Mike Mason — of "Bargain
   Basement"?
Mike Yes, that's right.
Policewoman (*from the phone*) Thought I recognized the voice. I'm a big
   fan of yours, Mike.
Mike Oh, thanks. (*He covers the mouthpiece*) This is all I need.
Policewoman (*from the phone*) Watch your show every week, regular as
   clockwork. Never miss it ... not once in eight years.
Mike Great ...
Policewoman (*from the phone*) Rotten luck about the award; saw it on TV.
Mike Is that right? (*He covers the mouthpiece, eyes to heaven. To Liz*) She
   saw the awards on TV.
Policewoman (*from the phone*) I must say, Mike, you was robbed. I think
   it was a total crime you didn't win.
Mike That makes two of us. Look, nice as it is talking to you, do you think
   you could send someone over?
Policewoman (*from the phone*) I'll get on to it right away, Mike.

Liz moves to the juke-box and touches it

Mike Thank you.
Policewoman (*from the phone*) Oh, and Mike — "Going, going, gone". (*She
   laughs*)

There is the sound of the phone being hung up

Mike (*hanging up too*) Up yours!
Liz (*looking at her hands, horrified*) Ahhhh!
Mike What is it?
Liz (*holding out her hands which are covered in blood. Shocked*) Blood —
   there's blood all over the juke-box!
Mike (*shocked*) What ... ?

*Mike switches on the spotlights which illuminate the alcove. Blood is
splattered on the juke-box and the surrounding wall. A large smear of blood
can be seen coming from behind the tapestry*

Picking up an article of clothing, Liz wipes the blood off her hands

Mike attempts to pull the tapestry aside; it falls to the floor. Behind the tapestry is the name "Carol Mitchell" written in blood, in large crude letters. A crumpled white dress, heavily stained with blood and streaked with mud, is nailed to the wall beneath the name

Mike stands transfixed at the sight of the dress and Carol Mitchell's name

Mike Christ!

Liz (*turning and seeing the dress and name*) Oh, my God! (*Hysterically*) Nobody knows, hey, Mike? No one can possibly connect us with Carol Mitchell's death. That's what you said, wasn't it? That's what you said ——

Mike (*to himself*) Jesus Christ!

Liz — all my imagination. Liz is cracking up. I knew this'd happen. I knew one day it'd all come out. Oh, God, what are we going to do?

Mike How did they get on to us?

Liz It's all your fault — you had to keep your name out of it, didn't you? You had to keep your goddamn name out of it.

Mike (*turning on her*) If anyone's to blame, it's you. You're the one who went back, remember. You're the one who said she was dead!

Liz I thought she was, Mike, I swear. Oh God, if only I hadn't panicked. If only I'd checked her properly ...

Mike (*interrupting*) If only I hadn't been nominated. If only she hadn't run out of petrol. If only we hadn't had too much to drink ...

Liz (*interrupting*) It was you that was drunk, Mike. You, not me. You're the one who insisted on driving.

Mike It was an accident.

Liz (*shouting*) You were drunk!

Mike For Chrissake, she's dead, Liz. Carol Mitchell's dead! Arguing about whose fault it was isn't going to change anything. (*He indicates the wall*) But why this? Why go to all this trouble?

Liz (*sobbing*) I knew this'd happen, I just knew it ...

Mike Liz, please, I'm trying to think.

Liz About what? You ran down a sixteen-year-old girl and didn't have the guts to report it. That's what they're going to say.

Mike Shut up!

Liz That's what they'll say, Mike. You ran down a sixteen-year-old girl and left her to die. Oh God, it's all going to come out.

Mike Nothing's going to come out.

Liz How can you say that?

Mike Because whoever did this can't prove a damn thing against us, that's why. No one even suspected us when it happened.

Liz Maybe they didn't then, but somebody certainly does now. Our name wasn't pulled out of a hat, Mike. Whoever did this knows that we killed Carol Mitchell ... You know what tomorrow is, don't you?

Mike Of course I know, I'm not stupid.

Liz Seven years to the day. That's not a coincidence, Mike. Someone knows.

Mike Maybe, but they can't prove it. If they couldn't seven years ago when it happened, what chance have they got now? The accident was nine miles away. The only thing that could've linked us to Carol Mitchell was the car, and we took care of that. (*Agitatedly*) But why this? First a telephone call and now this. (*After a pause; to himself*) Money! It's gotta be money. (*To Liz*) Whoever did this has got to be after money, otherwise they would've gone straight to the police. They're just trying to frighten us into believing they know more than they do. That's what this is all about. If they had any real proof they'd come out with it. They wouldn't have bothered with this nonsense ... No, no, they're just trying to panic us.

Liz Well, they've succeeded.

Mike Bastards! Well, they're not getting a cent out of me.

Liz fixes herself a drink during the following

They're gonna have to get in touch. I don't want you answering the telephone, the door, nothing. Just leave everything to me, understand? Everything. (*He sees Liz's drink*) And don't start on that.

Liz I need a drink.

Mike (*a sudden realization*) It was you, wasn't it?

Liz What ... ?

Mike That's how they know.

Liz What are you talking about?

Mike (*furious*) It was you! You opened your big mouth to someone about Carol Mitchell. You got drunk and opened your big mouth!

Liz Don't be ridiculous.

Mike Then how the hell did they find out? We're the only people who knew what happened that night. You and me! And I certainly haven't told anyone.

Liz Neither have I, Mike. I swear ...

Mike Jesus Christ, that's what happened. You got smashed and opened your big mouth.

Liz (*frightened*) No ...

Mike (*grabbing the glass out of her hand*) You stupid bitch, you've told somebody, haven't you? You've fucking gone and told somebody! (*He throws the drink in her face*)

There is a clatter; something has been knocked over outside

(*Stopping, suddenly alert*) What was that?

Liz What ... ?

Mike Sssssh! I heard something. Stay there. (*He switches the lights off, then looks out of the window*) There's someone out there.
Liz Oh, God!

Mike takes the hand gun out of the safe

Liz (*frightened*) What are you going? My God, what are you doing?
Mike I'll teach those bastards to mess with me.
Liz Mike, don't be stupid!
Mike (*clicking the gun closed*) Stay out of this.
Liz (*grabbing his arm*) Mike, please — you can't ...
Mike (*pulling free*) No one's going to blame me if I shoot an intruder. It's every citizen's right to protect his home and family. (*He moves to open the kitchen door*)

There is a loud knock at the front door

Mike and Liz freeze. They look at each other, mystified

(*A sudden realization*) It must be the police!
Liz The police ... ?
Mike I phoned them, remember?
Liz (*in a panic*) My God, the wall! They mustn't see the wall.
Mike Shit! (*He hides the gun under the sofa cushion and tries to re-hang the tapestry. Agitated, in a half whisper*) Well, don't just stand there, give me a hand!

They attempt to hang the tapestry

The knock is repeated

(*Calling out*) Be right with you.

Mike throws the tapestry to the floor, realizing there is no way they can do it

(*Half-whispered*) Shit! It's no good. (*He pulls down the white dress from the wall*)

There is another knock at the door

Mike heads for the door

Liz Don't answer it.

Mike I've got to answer it, they know I'm here!

Liz (*hysterical*) Oh, God, what are we going to do?

Mike (*thinking frantically*) I won't let them in — I'll tell them the call
must've been a hoax. There was no break-in .. (*He hands Liz the white
dress*) Dump it in the kitchen.

Liz exits into the kitchen

*Mike gets the gun from the sofa, switches on a table lamp, ruffles his hair and
puts on his dressing-gown. As he does so ——*

Liz enters, leaving the door ajar

Mike Liz! The lights!

Liz switches on the main room lights

No!

She switches them off again

(*Indicating the alcove*) Those, you stupid idiot! The alcove's!

Liz turns the main room lights back on and switches the alcove spotlights off

Liz What are you doing?

Mike (*ruffling his hair*) I've just woken up.

Liz But we've only just arrived home.

Mike I know that. I'm pretending. It's what I'm going to tell them.

Liz But the Awards. They saw you on TV. They know you've only just
arrived home.

Mike Shit!

There is another loud knock at the door

(*Calling out*) All right, all right, I'm coming.

Mike smoothes his hair, throws off the dressing-gown and composes himself

He exits to answer the front door, closing the porch door behind him

The front door is heard being unlocked

(*Off*) Sorry to keep you waiting.

The sentence is cut short by the sound of a shotgun blast

Mike crashes backwards through the porch door, which is heavily splattered with blood

Liz screams

Mike has taken the full blast of the shotgun in the stomach. His clothes are saturated in blood. His hands clutch at a terrible wound in his abdomen. As he tries to speak, blood bubbles from his mouth. Mike sways and falls into the room. He moans incoherently

Liz, self-preservation overcoming her terror, rushes to the porch door and slams it closed, gibbering with fear. She fumbles with the top bolt. As she does so ——

The large ring-handle begins to turn

She manages to shoot the bolt home just in time, then she shoots home the bottom bolt. The door is shaken violently. After a moment or two, the shaking stops

There is silence

Pause

Liz manages to control her sobbing, with an effort. She presses her ear against the door trying to hear what is going on outside. All is still

Mike (*weakly*) Liz ... Liz ...

Her desire to help Mike overcoming her fear of the unknown assailant, Liz kneels beside Mike and tries to staunch the flow of blood with an article of clothing from the floor

Carol Mitchell ...

All the lights go out; the only illumination now is the moonlight

Liz screams; then there is silence

Suddenly the silence is shattered by the sound of breaking glass as someone smashes the kitchen window

Liz makes a desperate bid to get to the kitchen door, but slips on some papers and falls. She scrambles to her knees; as she does so ——

The kitchen light comes on

Liz slams the door closed and locks it

Almost immediately there is a heavy pounding on the kitchen door as someone tries to force it open

Realizing the lock won't hold, Liz looks around desperately for something to wedge against the door. She drags furniture over and wedges it against the door. She pants, unable to get her breath

The pounding stops

Liz sinks to the floor, exhausted

Inexplicably, the curtains covering the french windows open

Liz Oh God!

One of the window panes smashes

Liz rushes to the french windows and closes and secures the inner wooden shutters. A sudden chest pain causes her to stagger momentarily before moving to Mike. She discovers he is dead

    Oh God!

The telephone rings. Liz runs and picks up the phone

    (*Into the phone, desperate, sobbing*) Help me! Please, help me. Someone's shot my husband. Somebody's killed Mike ... They're trying to get in.

The voice on the phone is the same as that heard earlier

Voice (*from the phone*) It's too late for help, Elizabeth. I'm already here.
Liz (*sobbing*) Oh, dear God ... Why are you doing this? What do you want?
Voice (*from the phone*) You, Elizabeth. I want you.
Liz Who are you?

Silence

(*Shouting*) Who are you?

The spotlight in the alcove slowly comes up on the name ...

Voice (*from the phone*) Carol Mitchell.
Liz (*sobbing*) But you can't be. You're dead ... You're dead ... (*A sudden sharp pain in her chest causes her to drop the receiver. She staggers, clutching her chest*) Ahhhh!
Voice (*sobbing in pain*) Help me ... Please ... Please, help me ... No, don't. Don't leave! Oh, God, please don't leave.

The caller starts crying helplessly; this continues during the following. The same voice is heard coming from different parts of the room. Soft at first, it grows steadily louder, jumbled, over-lapping: "Help me ... Don't leave me ... Please ... No, no, please don't ... " etc.. Suddenly the juke-box switches itself on and selects the record "Oh Carol", which it plays until it reaches the line, "I will surely die", where it sticks, repeating, "Die. Die. Die ... "

Liz backs away from the juke-box. As she does so ——

The rocking chair starts to rock. Books inexplicably spill from the bookcases and crash on to the floor. Mist seeps from the landing and swirls down the stairs

Liz screams

The shadowy figure of a woman appears at the head of the stairs

Liz stares at the woman, aghast

Mike slowly stands up behind Liz. He raises his hand, which is holding the gun

Mike (*cold, unemotional*) Elizabeth ...

Liz turns towards Mike. He shoots her

Liz falls to the floor; as she does so, there is silence and the lights snap to Black-out

ACT II
Scene 1

The same. The following morning. 7.00 a.m.

All evidence of the previous night's events has disappeared. The furniture is back in its rightful place. The dress, the writing and the blood that splattered the juke-box and wall have been removed. The broken china, papers and clothes have been cleared away. Except for a pile of books neatly stacked by the bookcase, it is as though nothing had ever happened

Darkness; then the lights come up

The room is in half-light, a shaft of sunlight streaming in from the landing window

Suddenly the few remaining books in the bookcase crash on to the floor

Mike enters winding up a ball of fishing twine which he follows to the bookshelf. (We see how the effect was achieved) He is dressed in casual clothes. He looks tired and drawn. He replaces the books, then opens the curtains and shutters on the french windows

A hammer used to smash the window can be seen hanging by a cord on the outside of the door. Mike unhooks it and puts it, along with the cord, into a sports bag on the sofa

Mike exits into the kitchen

After a moment, the rocking chair begins to rock

Mike enters, following some fishing twine to the rocking chair. He unfastens the twine and stuffs it into the bag

Mike goes upstairs, exits and re-enters with a cassette player which he inadvertently switches on. We hear the sobbing voice from the night before:

*"Help me ... Don't leave me ... " etc, coming from various parts of the room.
He unwinds the tape, unplugs the player and follows the leads to a loud
speaker and junction box behind the desk. Jumbling the speaker, box and
leads together, he puts them into the sports bag. He takes a J-cloth from his
pocket and starts cleaning the top of the juke-box*

Sue appears at the french windows. She is dressed in jeans and a top

Mike does not notice Sue

Sue sees Mike and taps on the window

Glancing uneasily up at the landing, Mike opens the french windows

Sue (*brightly*) Hi, Mike.
Mike Oh — er — hallo, Sue. (*He moves away, zipping up the sports bag*)
Sue Is it all right to come in?
Mike (*reluctantly*) Yeah ... yeah, of course. Bit early for you, isn't it, Sue?
Seven o'clock in the morning?
Sue Yeah, I couldn't sleep. (*She enters the room*)
Mike (*obviously uneasy*) You'll have to excuse me, I'm in a bit of a state.
I didn't get much sleep ... What can I do for you?
Sue (*putting her arms round Mike, suggestively*) I'll give you three guesses.
Mike Sue ...
Sue (*laughs*) Only joking. I just popped over to say how sorry I am about last
night.
Mike (*worried*) Last night ... ? Who told you?
Sue No one. I saw it on TV.

Mike looks at her, confused

The Awards.
Mike Oh, the Awards ... Sorry, I'm not really with it — I thought you meant
Liz.
Sue Liz ... ?
Mike She had to be admitted to Heathfield Clinic.
Sue (*shocked*) You're kidding — why? What happened?
Mike They think she's had a complete nervous breakdown. You saw what
she was like yesterday, right? Well that was nothing. She went absolutely
berserk. I couldn't believe it. Started smashing the place up. Threatened to
kill herself, kill me. It was horrendous.
Sue When?
Mike Last night when we got back. God knows what brought it on. She just

snapped. Honestly, I've never seen her like that before. She was really violent. Dr Campbell, the doctor from the Clinic, had to sedate her before they could take her in. She could be there for months.

Sue God, it must've been terrible for you.

Mike It was. It really was. I mean, I know things haven't been great between us, but even so, something like this ... I know it's the booze. I know that, it's really screwing her up but it doesn't make it any easier. If only she'd try and help herself. You can have all the Dr Campbells in the world but at the end of the day if she doesn't want to stop drinking there's nothing anyone can do about it. I feel so helpless.

Sue Poor Mike.

Mike Poor Liz — what with her heart and everything ...

Sue Yeah, absolutely.

Pause

(*Suggestively*) So you're on your own then?

Pause

Mike (*uneasily*) Er — yes.

Sue What a coincidence. So am I.

Mike Er — yes ... Listen, Sue ... I — er, look, please don't think I'm trying to be rude or anything ... but ...

Sue But what?

Mike (*flustered*) Well, it's just that I've got so much to do ...

Sue You want me to leave?

Mike No, no, of course I don't want you to leave ... It's just that ... Well, there's all Liz's things to sort out and everything ... You don't mind, do you, Sue?

Sue Yes, I'm heartbroken .. (*She laughs*) Course not. (*She puts her arms round him*) If there's anything I can do to help, Mike, you only have to ask.

Mike (*easing himself free*) Thanks, Sue, that's — er — very sweet of you, but honestly, I'll be fine.

Sue You sure?

Mike Absolutely.

Sue OK, but if there's absolutely anything I can do, anything at all, don't hesitate to ask. Promise?

Mike Promise.

Sue (*kissing him lightly on the lips*) Good.

Mike (*ushering her to the french windows*) I'll probably be tied up for the rest of the day what with one thing and another but after I've seen Liz I'll call and let you know how she's getting on.

At the french windows, Sue turns and faces Mike

Sue Mike, about last night.
Mike Yeah, what about last night?
Sue You don't think me being here had anything to do with it, do you?
Mike Liz's breakdown. No, no, absolutely not.
Sue Good.

Sue kisses Mike passionately. His response is somewhat less than half-hearted

(*Half-joking*) You're not getting tired of me, are you, Mike?
Mike (*insincerely*) Me ... ? Don't be daft.
Sue Good, because I'm certainly not getting tired of you ... (*she gives Mike a peck on the cheek*) even if you are twice my age. (*She heads off through the french windows*) Give Liz my love when you see her. Bye for now.

Sue exits

Mike Bye, Sue. (*He closes the french windows; to himself*) Shit!

Julie appears on the stairs. She is an extremely attractive and sophisticated woman in her forties. She is wearing Mike's dressing-gown

Julie (*coming down the stairs*) Who was that, Michael?
Mike (*wiping his mouth to remove any trace of lipstick. Flustered*) Oh — er — only the kid from next door, Sue Thompson. She popped over to commiserate about me not winning the award. I was frightened you were going to come down.
Julie (*going to him*) I'd hardly do that, would I?

Julie gives Mike a long, lingering kiss

(*Dreamily*) Mmmmm, just what the doctor ordered. (*She cups Mike's face in her hands*) God, you look terrible.
Mike Probably because that's how I feel.
Julie (*kissing Mike*) Poor darling.
Mike I told her about Liz. I said she'd become violent and had to be admitted to the Clinic.
Julie Good. The more disturbed we make her sound, the better. (*She heads for the kitchen*) I'm going to make some coffee, do you want a cup?
Mike No, not for me thanks, Julie.

Julie exits into the kitchen

(*Carrying a chair to the bookshelf nearest the french windows*) I wish they'd phone.

Julie (*off*) Sorry ... what did you say?

Mike (*standing on the chair; louder*) I said I wish the Clinic'd phone.

Julie (*off*) Give them time, it's only just after seven.

Mike You don't think anything's gone wrong, do you, Julie?

Julie (*off*) Like what?

Mike I don't know, anything.

Julie (*off*) How could it?

Mike (*reaching behind the books on the top shelf. To himself*) After last night ... very easily. (*He produces a a small loudspeaker from behind the books and places it in the sports bag*)

Julie enters carrying a mug of coffee

You are positive nobody saw you coming out of her room at the Clinic?

Julie (*deliberately*) Yes, Michael, I'm positive. Anyway, even if they did, I've every right to be there.

Mike (*reaching for another speaker*) This isn't how we planned it, Julie.

Julie But the result's the same.

Mike The result'd be the same if we'd blown her brains out.

Julie (*exasperated*) Michael ——

Mike (*climbing down with the speaker and putting it into the sports bag; interrupting*) We spent months planning it. Months. Going over every last detail. Rehearsing it again and again. Why? So we wouldn't miss anything that could incriminate us ... Now suddenly that's all out the window. Suddenly everything's changed.

Julie Nothing's changed; the only difference is she died at the Clinic instead of here ...

Mike (*in disbelief*) You call that nothing?

Julie (*deliberately*) Which actually might be to our advantage.

Mike Changing things on the spur of the moment is how mistakes are made.

Julie So what was I supposed to do? Let her come round? I had to sedate her.

Mike puts the bag into the cupboard under the stairs

Well, didn't I?

Mike (*agitated*) All I know is you said the shock'd kill her.

Julie I see.

Mike Well, you did. You said the state her heart was in, there was absolutely no way she'd survive. That's why we went to all this trouble: the writing on the wall; the phone calls; the blanks in the gun — because you said the shock'd bring on a heart attack.

Julie Which it did.

Mike But it didn't kill her, did it? I mean, what use is a goddamn heart attack if it's not fatal?

Julie With her medical history she should've dropped dead on the spot.

Mike You'd think for once in her damn life that woman'd be able to get something right. (*He looks at his watch*) Why don't they phone? They must've found her by now.

Julie Calm down. Everything'll be fine.

Mike I just hope to God we've done the right thing.

Julie You know we have.

Mike Do I ... ? Well, I'm not so sure.

Julie There was no alternative. If you'd divorced Elizabeth she would have gone straight to the police and told them about Carol Mitchell — even though it meant incriminating herself — just to spite you.

Mike We don't know that.

Julie Oh, come on.

Mike Well, we don't.

Julie She told you she would, Michael. She made that perfectly clear.

Mike Liz said a lot of things. She was all mouth.

Julie All right, for argument's sake, say she didn't. Elizabeth was an alcoholic. When she was drunk she had no idea what she was saying — she didn't even remember telling me about the accident. You know as well as I do it was only a matter of time before she blurted out the story to someone else. Anyway, whether we should have killed her's pretty academic. We did. (*She kisses him on the cheek*) Come on, relax. Everything'll be fine.

Mike I wish I had your confidence ...

Julie You finish clearing up and I'll get breakfast.

Mike Not for me thanks — I don't think I could hold anything down.

Julie kisses Mike

Sue appears beyond the french windows, crossing the garden, carrying a carrier bag

Julie (*seeing Sue*) Quick, that girl's coming back. Get rid of her.

Mike I thought I had.

Julie exits into the kitchen

Mike darts half-way up the stairs, turns and then makes his way down again. As he does so ——

Sue enters through the french windows

Mike Sue? ... What ...

Sue (*interrupting*) Bacon and eggs. I bet you haven't eaten. I'm right, aren't I?

Mike Sue, this is really sweet of you but I'm not hungry.

Sue You've got to eat, Mike — keep up your energy level.

Mike Sue, if I wanted to eat, I'm quite capable of fixing myself something.

Sue Oh yeah? I bet you can't even boil an egg. (*She heads for Mike*) I'm right, aren't I?

The juke-box bursts mysteriously into life and starts playing "Oh Carol" — Sue has obviously trodden on the carpet where Mike had hidden a foot switch

(*Startled*) How did that happen?

Mike (*moving to the juke-box, flustered*) There's a — er — loose wire somewhere. I've been meaning to ... (*He switches off the juke-box*)

Sue moves towards the kitchen

Sue, wait a minute ... Sue ...

Sue (*stopping*) Hey, I've just had a brilliant idea. How about breakfast in bed?

Mike (*deliberately*) I told you I am not hungry.

Sue (*putting her arms round Mike*) Me neither. We'll skip breakfast and go straight to bed.

Mike (*pushing her away, angrily*) Do you mind?

Sue (*taken aback*) What's wrong with you?

Mike What's wrong with me ... ? What the hell's wrong with you? My wife's just been admitted to hospital with a nervous breakdown.

Sue So?

Mike So ... ? Well, it's hardly the time to start leaping into bed, is it?

Sue (*laughing; disparagingly*) Ah, come on, Mike, not the "concerned husband routine", please. I think it's a bit late for that, don't you?

Mike Are you deaf or something? (*Deliberately*) Liz is in hospital.

Sue Oh, I see, it's OK to screw around when your wife's attending the Clinic, but not when she's actually in it ... Boy, you've got a really weird way of looking at things.

Mike Listen, sweetheart, I don't have to justify myself to you.

Sue Is that right?

Mike Yeah, that's right. I've already told you once, but so there can be no misunderstanding, I'll tell you again. I've got a lot to do. I'm not hungry. My wife's just been taken to hospital and I'd like to be on my own. I repeat, on my own. Got it? Good. Now if you don't mind ... (*He moves to usher Sue out*)

Sue (*picking up Julie's coffee mug*) Since when did you start wearing lipstick, Mike?

Mike What?

Sue (*holding the mug under his nose*) On the mug. Here, look! On the mug! Lipstick! You've got a woman here, haven't you? I'm right, aren't I? That's what this is all about. You've got a woman here! All that crap about being concerned for Liz — you just want to get rid of me so you can jump back into bed with your latest conquest. Who is it, Mike, anyone I know?

Mike (*very deliberately*) There's no one here.

Sue (*shouting*) Liar! (*She runs up the stairs*) Come out, come out, where ever you are.

Sue exits down the landing.

(*Off*) Don't be shy. Come out and say hallo.

Mike (*calling out*) Sue, there's no one up there, all right?

After a moment Sue appears at the head of the stairs carrying a woman's jacket

Sue (*coming down the stairs*) Very nice. And I suppose this is yours, is it Mike?

Mike (*grabbing the jacket*) No, it's Liz's.

Sue Liar!

Mike I'm getting her things together, remember?

Sue Liar! There's a woman here! (*She moves towards the kitchen*)

Mike (*grabbing Sue; angrily*) I told you there's no one here, all right? But let's get one thing straight: even if there was it'd be none of your damn business.

Sue I think the last six months have made it my "damn" business.

Mike (*disparaging*) I beg your pardon ... ?

Sue I said I think the last six months have made it my "damn" business.

Mike (*turning away*) Oh, go home.

Sue (*taken aback*) But, Mike ...

Mike Look, just piss off, Sue. All right? I don't need this kind of crap!

Sue Who the hell do you think you're talking to?

Mike You, sweetheart. Now get lost and don't bother coming back.

Sue That's it ... ? Just like that?

Mike (*weary*) Oh, go home.

Sue But the last six months, Mike. What about us?

Mike What about us? You were a bit on the side, love, that's all. Don't try and make it into some big romance.

Sue You bastard!

Mike (*controlled*) I think you'd better leave.

Sue Don't worry, I'm going! (*She crosses to the french windows, then turns to face Mike. Coldly*) You're going to regret this, Mike. Nobody uses me. Understand? By the time I'm finished, you're going to wish today never happened.

Mike Don't threaten me.

Sue Oh, that's not a threat. (*Mockingly*) You know something? You're not even good at it.

Mike At your age you shouldn't be in a position to know.

Sue Drop dead!

Sue exits, slamming the french windows behind her

Mike, highly agitated, locks the french windows and closes the shutters and curtains

Julie enters

During the following conversation, Mike dumps Sue's carrier bag in the kitchen, pulls back the rug and disconnects the foot-switch which is wired to the juke-box. He retrieves the sports bag from under the stairs, puts the switch into it and returns it to its place

Julie What was all that about?

Mike (*agitated*) It's all your fault. You're the one who told me to make a pass at the girl, remember? To hit on her to get Liz stressed out. Well, now it's all got out of hand. Everything's falling apart.

Julie What is?

Mike Everything! It's all going wrong. She set off the juke-box. She found your lipstick on the mug so she knows there's a woman here ...

Julie (*calm*) Michael ...

Mike God, we must be mad. I tell you, we're not going to get away with this.

Julie Michael, calm down.

Mike Don't you understand, the whole thing's falling apart.

Julie Nothing's falling apart. Honestly, I don't know what you're getting so excited about.

Mike (*in disbelief*) You're joking.

Julie Stop and think for a moment. Why on earth would anyone connect lipstick on a mug and a faulty juke-box with Elizabeth dying in hospital of a heart attack? Think about it. There's absolutely no connection.

Mike What if she saw us together?

Julie When?

Mike Just now, when she came over.

Julie Oh, come on, Michael. If she had, she'd have said something.

Mike All right, maybe she didn't. But she knows there's a woman here, Julie. She's not stupid. (*A sudden thought*) What if she connects it with the phone call?

Julie What phone call?

Mike She was here when you phoned.

Julie When?

Mike Yesterday, when you phoned about Liz.

Julie Why didn't you tell me?

Mike Because I didn't think it was important. But now she thinks there's a woman here ...

Julie Did you mention my name?

Mike I don't know ... I don't think so. I said you were my agent.

Julie Well, that's hardly incriminating, is it? A phone call from your agent.

Mike But she knows my agent. She's met him.

Julie Even if you did mention my name, the likelihood of her remembering it is so remote it's not worth worrying about.

The bleep of a telephone pager is heard

Julie looks at Mike for a moment then takes the pager from her dressing-gown pocket, switches it off, picks up the telephone and dials

Nurse (*from the phone*) Heathfield Rehabilitation Clinic. Nurse Woodhouse speaking. Can I help you?

Julie Helen, this is Dr Campbell. I've just been paged.

Nurse (*from the phone*) Oh, yes, Doctor — I'm afraid Mrs Mason died during the night.

Julie Died? When?

Nurse (*from the phone*) Well, we followed your instructions not to wake her till after morning rounds to give the sedative a chance to wear off, so we can't be sure of the exact time.

Julie Has the cause of death been established?

Nurse (*from the phone*) Dr Gilbert's certain it was a heart attack.

Julie Heart attack, I see ... All right, Helen, I'll be in later this morning. In the meantime, could you break the news to Mr Mason and make the necessary arrangements? Oh, and you'd better tell him I'll drop by to see him on my way to the Clinic. He'll probably need a sedative.

Nurse (*from the phone*) Certainly.

Julie Thank you, Helen. Goodbye. (*She hangs up and smiles*) You are now a widower — unofficially, of course.

Mike No snags?

Julie None whatsoever. They're convinced it was a heart attack. I told you there was nothing to worry about.

Mike (*sighs*) God, what a relief. (*A sudden thought*) There won't be an autopsy, will there?

Julie Why should there be? People die of heart attacks every day. Anyway, even if there was they wouldn't find anything. Air injected into the vein doesn't leave a trace. I told you, it's undetectable. It'll simply look as though she had a heart attack, and with her medical history, no one'll look any further.

The telephone rings. Mike goes to answer it

Let it ring for a moment.

Mike waits, then picks up the receiver. He holds it for a moment while he gets into the right frame of mind. He takes a deep breath

During the following, Julie exits into the kitchen

Mike (*into the phone*) Hallo.

Nurse (*from the phone*) Can I speak to Mr Mason, please?

Mike Speaking.

Nurse (*from the phone*) Mr Mason, this is the Heathfield Rehabilitation Clinic. I'm afraid I've some bad news concerning your wife.

Mike (*concerned*) Liz ... ? What's happened? Is she all right?

Nurse (*from the phone*) I'm afraid your wife has suffered a fatal heart attack, Mr Mason.

Mike (*shocked*) Oh, my God!

Nurse (*from the phone*) I'm very sorry. If it's any comfort, she would have felt no pain.

Mike Oh, no.

Nurse (*from the phone*) I'm terribly sorry, Mr Mason. Please accept our condolences.

Mike So — er — so what happens now? What do I do? Do I come in?

Nurse (*from the phone*) Well, if you'd find it less distressing we could make all the immediate arrangements for you.

Mike Could you? It'd be appreciated. I really don't feel ...

Nurse (*from the phone*) I understand. Obviously, there are certain details we'll need to discuss ... Could you call in tomorrow?

Mike Yes, yes, of course.

Nurse (*from the phone*) Shall we say three o'clock?

Mike Yes, that'd be fine.

Nurse (*from the phone*) Oh, and Dr Campbell asked me to tell you she'll be dropping in sometime this morning.

Mike Thanks.

Nurse (*from the phone*) Once again, please accept our deepest sympathy.
Mike Thank you very much. (*He replaces the receiver; to himself*) Going,
  going, gone! (*He breaks into a broad smile; calling out*) Now it's official.

*There is a loud pop from off stage and a champagne cork flies through the
kitchen door and across the room*

Julie enters carrying an open bottle of champagne and two glasses

Mike Champagne?
Julie (*pouring a glass of champagne*) I think this calls for a small celebration,
  don't you? After all, it's not everyday you lose a patient.
Mike It's not every day you lose a wife.

Julie hands Mike the glass and pours another

  (*Raising his glass*) To you, my love, whose inventiveness and coolness
  under pressure made it all possible.

Julie raises her glass

  And to Liz for bringing us together. About the only good thing she ever did.
Julie To us and the future.
Mike I'll drink to that.

They drink

  Everything worked out exactly as you said it would.
Julie Remember, leave it for a couple of days, phone the Clinic, say you're
  depressed, make an appointment to see me ——
Mike (*interrupting*) And during the treatment, love blossoms. (*He puts his
  arms round Julie and kisses her*) You, my love, are unique. Not only are
  you intelligent, resourceful, cool and sophisticated, but you're incredibly
  sexy with it. (*He kisses her*) What time are you due at the Clinic?
Julie About nine — why?
Mike We-e-ll, I was just wondering if you could, you know, be persuaded
  to make it ten. (*He kisses her*)
Julie You've just talked me into it.

*They head for the stairs. As they pass the telephone table, Julie hands Mike
the bottle and takes the phone off the hook*

Mike What're you doing?

Julie (*putting her arm round his waist*) We don't want to be disturbed, do
    we?

Mike Like I said, you think of everything. (*He starts up the stairs*)

Julie watches Mike go up the stairs. The lights fade to Black-out

SCENE 2

The same. Late that afternoon

The curtains and shutters are open

The Lights come up

*After a moment, Julie enters from the kitchen carrying a tray with a coffee pot,
cream jug, sugar bowl and two cups and saucers on it. She is dressed in
fashionable trousers and top. She places the tray on the coffee table and
pours herself a cup of coffee. As she does so ——*

There is a knock at the door

Julie exits into the porch

The front door is heard opening

Julie (*off*) You must be Sue Thompson. Please, won't you come in.

Sue enters. She is wearing the same dress as in Act I, Scene 1

The front door is heard closing

Julie enters

I appreciate you coming over like this at such short notice, Miss Thompson.

Sue That's all right. You said it was important. (*She looks around*) Where's
    Mr Mason?

Julie Upstairs sleeping. By the way, I'm Dr Campbell, from the Heathfield
    Rehabilitation Clinic. Mrs Mason's therapist.

Sue Yes, I know.

Julie Really?

Sue I saw you once when you came to pick up Liz.

Julie Oh right. Please, won't you sit down.

They sit

Cup of coffee? I've just made a fresh pot.
Sue Er — yeah, thanks.
Julie (*pouring a cup of coffee*) Cream and sugar?
Sue Just cream, please.

Julie pours the cream and hold the cup out to Sue

What is it you want to speak to me about? (*She takes the cup*) Thanks. You
said on the phone it was important.
Julie Actually, it's about Mrs Mason.
Sue Liz?
Julie I don't suppose you've heard but she had to be admitted to the Clinic
late last night.
Sue Er — yes. Actually Mr Mason told me.
Julie He did? When?
Sue This morning. I dropped by to — er — say how sorry I was he didn't
win the award. He said she had to be sedated before you could take her in.
Julie That's right, yes. The poor woman had a complete breakdown.
Sue Mike ... Mr Mason said. How terrible.
Julie Unfortunately there were complications.
Sue Nothing serious I hope?
Julie I'm afraid Mrs Mason suffered a heart attack. She died early this
morning.
Sue (*shocked*) Liz is dead ... ? My God, I can't believe it.
Julie It's a tragedy, though I suppose with her medical history it was always
a possibility.
Sue You mean her heart condition?
Julie (*surprised*) You knew about that?
Sue Yeah, Mike said she had to take some kind of pills.
Julie That's right. To bring down her blood pressure.
Sue How's he taking it?
Julie Not terribly well. I've given him a sedative to make him sleep.
Sue (*getting to her feet*) Well, thanks for letting me know. If you could tell
Mike how sorry I am.
Julie Were you aware Mrs Mason knew of your relationship with her
husband?
Sue (*taken aback*) I beg your pardon?
Julie Did you know Elizabeth knew you were having an affair with her
husband?
Sue What the hell are you talking about?
Julie Please. I've already spoken to Mr Mason. He's told me the whole story.

Pause

Sue No, not that I think it's any of your business, but no, I wasn't aware Liz knew ... This wasn't just a casual affair.

Julie But that's all it was to Mr Mason, wasn't it?

Sue What?

Julie A casual affair. According to him you couldn't accept that. That's why he wanted to call it off.

Sue That's not true ...

Julie He said you started making abusive phone calls, threatening to tell his wife ——

Sue Oh, please ...

Julie — and on the night Mrs Mason had her breakdown, you came by to try and patch things up.

Sue No!

Julie And you were still here when she came back and there was a violent argument.

Sue That is absolute garbage! I'm sorry, I don't want to talk about this any more. (*She moves to the door*) Whatever happened between Mr Mason and myself has got absolutely nothing to do with you.

Julie Actually, Elizabeth's death isn't quite as straightforward as it first appeared.

Sue stops in her tracks

There's no doubt it was a heart attack that killed her, but I'm of the opinion it was induced.

Sue (*confused*) I'm sorry ... ?

Julie Induced; I believe somebody administered something to bring on the attack.

Sue (*horrified*) On purpose ... ? But that's murder.

Julie Exactly.

Sue I can't believe it. Why on earth would anyone want to kill Liz?

Pause

Julie A young woman was seen in the grounds of the Clinic late last night.

Sue So? Hey, wait a minute, you're not insinuating I had anything to do with it, are you? Because if you are ——

Julie I'm just stating the facts, Sue. A young woman was seen in the grounds of the Clinic last night.

Sue Yeah, well, it wasn't me, all right? I'd never do anything to hurt Liz. I don't even know what a heart attack's supposed to look like, let alone how to cause one. Look, I don't know what Mike's told you about me, but he's lying.

Julie Why should he lie?

Sue Why? Why do you think? To implicate me. That's why.

Julie What would he gain by that?

Sue I would've thought that was pretty obvious. To take the attention away from himself. Everyone knew they didn't get along. He couldn't stand the sight of her. If anyone had a reason to kill Liz, it was Mike.

Julie But Mr Mason couldn't possibly have killed his wife. The Clinic phoned him here at the house about the time she must have died.

Sue Then he's lying to protect someone else.

Julie Who?

Sue I don't know. All I know is I didn't do it, and if he's making up lies about me, it must be to protect someone else.

Julie But who?

Sue I don't know!

There is a pause

(*Looking up*) There was a woman here this morning. When I came round to see Mike. I didn't actually see her, but there was somebody here. I'm certain of it.

Julie You've no idea who it was?

Sue No. (*Desperately*) Look, I realize it sounds as if I'm just trying to shift the blame, but I swear it's the truth, I'm not making it up. I'm sure there's another woman involved that he's trying to protect.

There is a pause

Julie (*thoughtfully*) You could be right. When I brought some tranquillizers to Mr Mason this morning I got the same impression.

Sue That someone was here?

Julie Yes. I could've sworn I heard somebody moving round upstairs. I must say he was very quick to point the finger at you when I told him of our misgiving over Elizabeth's death. Almost eager in fact. Elizabeth told me she'd been getting strange phone calls, someone calling and then hanging up without speaking.

Sue I know. It happened when I was here last night. There was a big argument about it. Liz thought it was some woman for Mike. Apparently it was the fourth time it's happened this week — wait a minute, there was an earlier call, just before Liz got back.

Julie From whom?

Sue Some woman. Mike mentioned her name during conversation but I'm damned if I can remember it. Jane ... Judy ... he said it was his agent. But it couldn't have been. His agent's name's Harry something or other. I met him. If there wasn't something going on between them, why would he lie about it? ... Julie?

Julie Pardon?

Sue Julie! That was the name of the woman Mike was talking to.

Julie Are you positive?

Sue Yes. I remember now. It was definitely Julie.

Julie (*thoughtfully*) Julie Robertson!

Sue He didn't mention her surname.

Julie No, Julie Robertson. She's a nurse at the Clinic ... Of course! She was the one who reported seeing the young woman in the grounds last night.

Sue A nurse? So she'd know how to bring on a heart attack.

Julie Exactly. I think we're going to have to get in touch with the police. You don't mind talking to them, do you?

Sue No, of course not.

Julie (*looking for the number*) My God, everything falls into place. It was Julie Robertson who supposedly phoned Mike at home.

Julie dials. Through the speaker we hear the talking clock, which continues throughout the following conversation

(*Into the phone*) Hallo, this is Dr Campbell from the Heathfield Clinic. I'm afraid one of my patients has died under what we consider very suspicious circumstances. ... Mrs Elizabeth Mason. ... No, I'm sorry, I really don't think I can discuss that over the phone — I'm not at the Clinic but I could be there in fifteen minutes. ... There's someone else I think you should talk to. A Miss Thompson. ... Right, I'll bring her with me to the Clinic ... Goodbye. (*She hangs up*) Right, I'll just get my bag. (*A sudden thought*) Oh, do you need to call anyone and let them know where you'll be?

Sue No, it's OK, my parents are away for the weekend.

Julie Good. (*She heads up the stairs*) Have you told anyone?

Sue What? About Mike and I?

Julie Yes.

Sue Hardly. An affair with a married man isn't something you broadcast — especially him being a celebrity and everything.

Julie exits. She re-enters moments later, wearing the jacket Sue found that morning. In one hand she has a wad of cotton wool soaked in chloroform and in the other hand, a medical case, which she puts down

I mean, if the papers got hold of it, they'd —— (*She recognizes the jacket and falters*) That jacket. Oh my God, it was you ...

Julie drops the case. Sue tries to get to her feet. Julie is on her, forcing the cotton wool over her nose and mouth. Sue struggles desperately. After a moment she stops kicking

Julie strokes Sue's cheek. As she does so, the Lights fade to Black-out

SCENE 3

The same. Late that night

The curtains are closed

Julie sits, as yet unseen, in the rocking chair, dead, her head thrown back, her mouth hanging open, her eyes staring sightlessly at the ceiling. Her throat has been cut and blood saturates her dress. She is covered with a dustsheet

Darkness. The telephone is ringing

The Lights come up. The only illumination is moonlight through the gap in the curtains

After a long pause a Light is switched on upstairs and spills on to the landing

Mike appears on the stairs dressed in pyjamas, yawning. He appears groggy and half asleep. He descends the stairs

Mike (*mumbling*) All right, all right. (*He picks up the telephone. Into the phone, groggily*) Hallo? Hallo?
Voice (*a girl's; from the phone*) Mike?
Mike Who is this?
Voice (*from the phone*) How did you enjoy my present?
Mike What?
Voice (*from the phone*) I left you a present, Mike. A little surprise.
Mike What the hell are you talking about? Who is this?
Voice (*from the phone*) It's on the rocking chair. A goodbye present.
Mike Is that you, Sue? For Chrissake, it's the middle of the night.
Voice (*from the phone*) I hope you enjoy it, Mike. A little something to remember me by.

The line goes dead

Mike Hallo ... Hallo. (*He hangs up and switches on a small table lamp. He sees the dustsheet-covered body. Shocked*) Christ! (*He crosses to the chair, horrified. He stands staring at it for a moment. Then, terrified at what he will find, he gingerly removes the dust sheet. He recoils in horror*) Oh, my God!

The telephone rings. Mike grabs it

Voice (*from the phone*) I'm coming for you, Mike.

The phone goes dead

Terrified, Mike replaces the phone and dashes frantically to the safe where the gun is kept. He scrabbles desperately, searching for it

Mike Where is it? Where the hell is it? (*He rushes to the desk, panic-stricken, and searches through the drawers. He is unable to find the gun. He looks round in desperation*)

Julie's hand shoots out and grabs Mike by the wrist. Mike screams and recoils in horror

　Liz rushes on from between the curtains of the french windows, wielding a meat cleaver

Liz brings the cleaver down with all her force on Mike, slicing into his right shoulder. He screams in agony and wheels round. He clutches at his shoulder then looks at the blood on his hand

Julie coldly watches the attack that follows

Liz (*viciously*) Going to murder me, were you, Mike? (*She strikes out at him again*)

Mike recoils, staggering behind the sofa. Liz follows him around the room, slashing with the cleaver. Mike backs into the kitchen door. Liz strikes out again, narrowly missing Mike; the cleaver sinks into the woodwork. Liz strikes again; as she does so, Mike ducks and slips, falling against the rocking chair. Liz hacks at his back before he can get away. Mike screams, writhing on the floor in agony

Liz Is that what you were going to do? Frighten poor old Liz to death?
Mike (*hardly able to talk*) But ... the phone call ... the Clinic ...
Liz It was me, Mike. The actress who made her career out of auditions. (*Nurse Woodhouse's voice*) If it's any comfort she would've felt no pain. (*In her normal voice*) Unlike you, my precious.

Liz hits Mike viciously on the leg. He screams

Julie moves to Mike, removing the latex mould of a wound from her throat

Julie They're going to find you hacked to pieces. The victim of some crazed psychopath you obviously disturbed robbing the place.

Liz And thanks to you, I've got the perfect alibi. Poor drunken Liz, pushed to the brink by your womanizing, was eight miles away at the Clinic, having a nervous breakdown. Under sedation.

Julie Being checked every two hours by that kind, dedicated Dr Campbell. The woman who loves you. The woman willing to risk everything, just for the chance of being with you.

Liz And you believed it. You're so conceited. She despises you, Mike.

Julie You disgust me!

Liz (*smugly*) It was all planned. Everything. From the very beginning.

Julie The idea for Liz's heart attack.

Liz The way it went wrong ... It was an act to get me out of the house. We drugged your champagne so you couldn't go out.

Julie I took the phone off the hook so you couldn't mention Liz's death if someone called.

Liz You didn't even question my weak heart—I've never had a weak heart.

Julie The only difficult part was pretending to enjoy your sordid love-making. It made my flesh crawl just being near you. Well, the charade is over, Michael. You're going to die!

Mike (*to Liz*) Please, don't do this.

Julie She wants revenge, Mike. For the way you've used her these last seven years. Manipulating her. Chipping away at her self-confidence until you knew she'd be so dependent on you she could never leave.

Liz As long as I was your wife, you were safe.

Julie She couldn't testify against you, could she, Michael? She couldn't tell the truth about Carol Mitchell. That's the only reason you didn't divorce her.

Mike That's not true ...

Liz God, you must think I'm so stupid. (*She makes as though to hit him*)

Mike Liz, please don't ...

Julie You brought this on yourself. We were just going to blackmail you. Squeeze you for every penny.

Liz But you left me no choice, Mike. You were going to kill me ... After everything we'd gone through together, you were going to kill me.

Liz hits Mike on the left shoulder. He screams

Mike (*whimpering*) Liz ... It was her ... she's the one who said ...

Julie (*frenzied*) Liar! You wanted her dead!

Mike (*pleading*) Liz, please ...

During the following dialogue, Mike, in a pitiful attempt to get away, half crawls, half drags himself across the floor, whimpering. The effort is too much for him and he collapses by the french windows. Liz and Julie follow him

Julie Why should she pity you? You were going to murder her.
Mike It was Julie ...
Julie Liar!
Mike She's using you, Liz. She's after the money.
Liz That's right. Julie needs the money and I need to be rid of you. Your death's the perfect solution.

During the following dialogue, Mike, still trying to escape, drags himself behind the sofa

Julie You thought you were so clever, didn't you, Michael? Well, now she'll have everything.
Mike Don't ... please don't. Can't you see what she's done?
Julie (*frenzied*) Kill him!
Mike She's used us both. Turned us against each other.
Julie Kill him!

Liz raises the cleaver

Mike Liz, please ...

Liz hesitates

Julie Kill him! Kill him! Kill him!

Liz brings the cleaver down with all her force. Mike's scream is cut short. Liz goes berserk, hitting his unseen body again and again, until she stops, exhausted. She is splattered in blood. She stands looking down at him, breathing heavily. After a moment, she starts sobbing uncontrollably

Liz Oh, my God ... Oh, my God ... (*She drops the cleaver*)
Julie It's all right, Elizabeth, it's over.
Liz (*distraught*) We had to do it, Julie. We had to ... (*She continues to sob under the following*)
Julie (*producing a pair of gloves and putting them on*) You had no choice, Elizabeth. He was going to murder you. (*She fills a large tumbler with whisky*) If we're going to get back to the Clinic before you're missed, we've got to be out of here within ten minutes. (*She hands the whisky to Liz*) Come on, drink this.

Liz gulps down half the glass

Liz I can't believe I've done it, Julie — I can't ...

Julie If he'd disturbed someone ransacking the place, it'd be in a shambles. We've got to make it look as though there's been a struggle —— (*she begins to mess up the room systematically, upturning chairs, sweeping ornaments off the shelves, etc., during the following*) — as though he put up a fight.

Liz (*sobbing*) If only I'd confronted him, told him I knew — maybe it wouldn't have come to this.

Julie There's no need to feel guilty, Elizabeth. He deserved it. He was prepared to murder you. It's only right, he had to die. Where's the phone and the cassette?

Liz The what?

Julie The phone and the tape you used to wake Michael. Where did you leave them?

Liz Outside.

Julie exits through the french windows

(*Off*) As soon as the insurance comes through, I'll give you the money for the Clinic.

Julie enters with a mobile phone, a hand-held cassette player, and a carrier bag

I'm not interested in the money.

Liz (*confused*) What do you mean?

Julie Just that: I'm not interested in the money, Elizabeth. Lock the windows and close the curtains. (*She puts the blood-stained dustsheet and latex mask into the carrier bag*) Come on, come on. Give me the key. Come on, we've got to hurry. (*During the following she takes out Mike's gun and points it at Liz*)

Liz opens the porch door and screams

Sue Thompson falls into the room at Liz's feet, gagged and trussed up with carpet tape. She is wearing a white slip

Liz (*turning to Julie. Shocked*) Julie, what's going on? (*She sees Julie pointing Mike's gun at her*) Oh, my God.

Julie Move away from the door! Move away from the door! No one's going to doubt for a moment when they discover their mutilated bodies that you killed them in a fit of jealous rage and then, filled with remorse, took your

own life. (*She indicates the rocking chair with the gun*) Sit in the chair,
Elizabeth.

Liz (*almost paralysed with fear*) Oh God, no ...

Julie (*pointing the gun at Liz*) In the chair.

Liz No, Julie ... Please ...

*Julie fires the gun, shattering the plate hanging on the wall next to Liz's head.
Liz sits in the chair, cowering*

Liz (*sobbing*) Oh God, Julie ... What are you doing? Why are you doing this?

Julie takes a roll of carpet tape from her bag and tosses it on to Liz's lap

Julie Tape your ankles together.

Liz (*confused*) What ... ?

Julie Tape your ankles together.

Liz Julie, please ...

Julie (*jabbing the gun in the back of Liz's neck; screaming*) Do it!

Liz starts taping her ankles together, whimpering with fear

Julie While you were building what you thought was your cast-iron alibi,
you were simply playing into my hands

Liz finishes securing her ankles

Break the tape.

Liz complies

Now tape your left arm to the chair.

Liz tapes her left wrist to the arm of the chair during Julie's next speech

Every scene, every contrived jealous outburst brought you one step closer
to your death.

Liz finishes securing her wrist

Break the tape.

Liz leans forward and tears the tape with her teeth

(*Taking the roll of tape from Liz*) Now the right arm. (*She tapes Liz's right wrist to the chair*) So you see, Elizabeth, thanks to your flawless performance everyone is convinced you are mentally unstable. Capable of anything. (*She walks behind Liz*)

Liz (*terrified*) Why are you doing this? ... What are you going to do?

Julie (*producing a mobile phone*) Phone the police, of course. (*She dials, then covers Liz's mouth with her free hand*)

Policeman (*from the phone*) Burgess Hill Police Station.

Julie (*into the phone, sounding normal*) This is Dr Campbell at the Heathfield Clinic. One of my patients, a Mrs Elizabeth Mason, is missing. She was admitted last night in a very disturbed state of mind. She'd been making violent threats against her husband and a number of young women. In my opinion, in her present condition, she could be dangerous. I've tried to contact Mr Mason but unfortunately his number's unobtainable. I wonder if you could possibly send an officer round to make sure everything's all right? The address is 120 Woodbridge Drive.

Policeman (*from the phone*) I'll send someone over as soon as I can, Doctor.

Julie And if you would phone me here at the Clinic and let me know the outcome, I'd appreciate it.

Policeman (*from the phone*) Of course.

Julie That's the Heathfield Clinic, extension 341.

Policeman (*from the phone*) Right, Doctor. Thank you.

Julie Good-night. (*She hangs up*) You can't murder a person in cold blood, Elizabeth, and expect to go unpunished.

Liz But it was your idea to kill Mike — you told me to! You planned it all, Julie. You said ——

Julie (*screaming*) Not that scum! (*Calmly*) Carol Mitchell.

Liz (*confused*) Carol Mitchell?

Julie You murdered her, Elizabeth.

Liz Murdered her ... ? For God's sake, Julie, it was an accident ... I wasn't even driving.

Julie It was an accident until you left her. Then it became cold-blooded murder.

Liz I only left her because I thought she was dead.

Julie But she wasn't, was she, Elizabeth. Carol Mitchell wasn't dead.

Liz It was dark. I'd never have left her if I'd known she was alive.

Julie But you thought she was dead.

Liz Yes.

Julie Is that what you really thought?

Liz Yes! You know it is! I told you!

Julie And what exactly did you tell me, Elizabeth?

Liz (*bewildered*) What do you mean ... ?

Julie What did you tell me? That afternoon you came to the Clinic and bared
your soul in an attempt to exorcise your guilt? What did you tell me? ...
Well, come on, Elizabeth. I'm waiting. (*She gets more and more agitated,
forcing Liz's head forward with the gun, screaming in her ear*) What did
you tell me? (*Quiet. Controlled*) You don't remember, do you, Elizabeth?
No, of course you don't. How could you? You were so drunk, the next day
you couldn't even remember being there, let alone what you'd said.

Liz But, you told me ——

Julie What I wanted you to think I knew. That afternoon, you told me
everything. Every last detail. You didn't for one minute think Carol
Mitchell was dead. She was conscious when you went back ——

Liz No.

Julie — she asked you for help and you walked away ——

Liz That's not true.

Julie (*putting the gun to Liz's head*) — left her lying there. Crying. Begging
for help ...

Liz No, no, please don't ... Oh God, don't ...

Julie What's it feel like, Elizabeth? How does it feel to be totally helpless?

Liz Oh God, please ...

Julie It was eight hours before she was found. Eight hours. Lying there.
Unable to move. Waiting to die ... Can you imagine the pain she must've
gone through because of you? How she must've suffered?

Liz (*almost incoherent*) Don't, don't. Please — don't ...

Julie (*taking the gun away from Liz's head*) It's all on tape, Elizabeth. I
record all my sessions. Do you want to hear it? How she was crying,
begging for help ... Those are your words, Elizabeth, not mine. (*She
switches the tape on*)

Liz's voice (*from the cassette player. Very drunk*) I didn't even see her ...
I remember the car hitting something, then we stopped ... Mike just sat
there. He kept saying "Christ, we've hit somebody" over and over
again ... (*She sobs*)

Julie's voice (*from the player*) Then what happened?

Liz's voice (*from the player*) Mike got out and told me to stay in the car ...
but I followed him back along the road ... then we saw her. Mike panicked
and ran back to the car shouting at me to get back in. I started to go back
and then I heard her.

Julie's voice (*from the player*) Heard her? ...

Julie (*ramming the cassette player against Liz's face. Shouting, over the
tape*) So you thought she was dead, did you, Elizabeth? You thought she
was dead.

Liz's voice (*from the player*)... the car had knocked her into the ditch ... it was
terrible. She was just lying there ... looking up at me ...

Julie You knew she was alive?

Liz's voice (*from the player*) ... Oh God, God, there was so much blood ...

Julie Carol Mitchell ... you knew she was alive?

Liz's voice (*from the player*) She kept saying "Help me ... please help me" ... she couldn't move ...

Julie (*switching off the tape and taking the cassette out of the player*) So you just walked away.

Liz Oh, God ...

Julie Why didn't you phone and let somebody know where she was? You didn't have to give your name.

Liz I couldn't.

Julie That's all it would've taken. One simple telephone call and Carol would be alive today.

Liz (*breaking down*) She might've recognized us, told the police who we were.

Julie So you left her to die.

Liz We'd have lost everything — everything. Mike's show had just taken off. If it had come out he'd run someone down when he was drunk he'd have lost his job. We'd have lost everything. Everything we'd worked for. The house ... everything.

Julie So you left her to die. Sixteen years old, with her whole life ahead of her, and you left her to die. (*Controlled*) The doctor said if they had got her to hospital even an hour earlier, they could have saved her. An hour earlier and Carol would be alive today ... Oh, Michael may have run her down, but you killed her. When you walked away you murdered her as surely as if you'd put a gun to her head and pulled the trigger. (*She cocks the gun*) Well, Michael received his just deserts, now it's your turn. (*She puts the gun to Liz's head*)

Liz No, please ...

Julie pulls the trigger. The hammer falls on an empty chamber

Julie Seven years I've waited for this. Seven years to the day, to the hour. (*She takes a clock from her bag and places it in front of Liz*) The alarm is set for four fifteen, the time Carol Mitchell died. The time you're going to die.

Liz Oh God, Julie, why? Why?

Julie Because Carol Mitchell was my daughter. You murdered my daughter. It was me that found her — I found my daughter lying in a ditch. Covered in blood. She didn't recognize me — she didn't even know who I was. Her own mother. The police said the driver must've known the area. Carol's car had broken down and she was walking along the Old Clayton Road, a back road that only locals would've known about. The police contacted every garage and bodyshop in the district, but they drew a blank; after a while, they stopped looking. But I didn't, Elizabeth. I never gave up. I spent every spare moment driving to shopping centres, cinemas, scouring the car parks for damaged cars; I contacted insurance companies, answered secondhand car ads ... I tried to put Carol's death behind me — I tried, but I couldn't; I kept seeing her lying there, my baby, lying there — and then I found it! I was going through back issues of local newspapers, and there it was. "Four days after failing to win a BAFTA, local celebrity, Mike Mason, suffered a second blow when his new BMW was stolen from his home in Westmeston. It was later discovered, burnt out, ten miles away on the Downs." Burnt out. What better way of getting rid of the evidence. The deeper I dug, the more everything pointed to you and Mike. The award ceremony was on the same night as the accident. Driving back to Westmeston, you would've come off the A23 at Pyecombe, which meant you would've driven past the Old Clayton Road. You would've known that by taking it, you'd cut three miles off your journey. Everything started falling into place. I found out all I could about you and Mike, Elizabeth: I joined your golf club, befriended you, gained your confidence, persuaded you to attend the Clinic ... When you confessed, I could've gone straight to the police, played them the tape — but what would you have got? Two years at the most. Two years for my daughter's life. No, you both had to suffer the way Carol suffered.

The alarm clock goes off

Liz struggles desperately to break free

In her mind, Julie hears the cries of her daughter from the scene of the accident. Carol uses the same words that were on the tape. Carol's voice has a strange, echoey quality about it

Carol's voice (*through speakers. Sobbing*) Help me ... please, help me ... Don't leave ... Please, don't leave me ... *etc.*

Julie cocks the gun and slowly points it at Liz's head. Liz sobs, begging incoherently

Carol's voice fades

Julie falters. She lowers the gun. It looks as though she is unable to go through with it after all

Carol's voice comes through the speakers; it is joined by Julie's voice from the cassette, building to a crescendo

Carol's voice (*through speakers. Sobbing*) Don't leave ... please, please, don't leave me... Oh, God ... help me ... Please help me ... *etc.*

Julie's voice (*on cassette*) And you just walked away ... You just walked away ... You just walked away ... You just walked away ... *etc.*

Compelled by the voices, Julie raises the gun and fires. Liz's head is spun sideways by the impact of the bullet. Blood from the wound splatters on to the wall behind her

Simultaneously, the voices stop. The alarm continues to ring

Putting the gun down, Julie takes a knife from the drinks cabinet and, cutting the tape from Liz's wrists and ankles, places the gun into Liz's lifeless hand. Switching off the alarm, she puts the clock and cassette into the bag. She then drags Sue, struggling, across the room to the front of the sofa. As Sue struggles, the gag slips from her mouth

Sue (*sobbing*) Don't, don't ... Please, don't hurt me ... Leave me alone. Please, leave me alone ...

For a moment, Carol's voice is heard merging with Sue's

Carol's voice (*through speakers*) Don't ... Please, don't leave me ... don't ...

Julie stops, confused

Carol's voice fades

Leaving Sue whimpering in terror, Julie moves behind the sofa and picks up the blood-stained cleaver

Sue Oh, God ... Don't hurt me ... Please, don't hurt me.

Julie (*looking down at Sue; dazed*) I have to. If you don't die, it wouldn't make sense: you have to die at the same time as the others.

Sue's and Carol's voices mingle during the following

Sue Oh, my God, don't ... Don't ... Please ... Please, don't ... Leave me alone ... Please, leave me ... *etc.*

Carol's voice Don't ... Don't ... Please, don't leave me ... *etc.*

Julie can no longer differentiate between the voices

Carol's voice continues throughout the scene, getting louder, then softer, then louder again

The Lights fade during the following, focusing on the helpless figure of Sue. Julie moves towards her. She raises the cleaver. As she does so ——

The sound of a speeding police car is heard in the distance

Julie falters. A look of apprehension crosses her face

The sound of the approaching car grows louder. A sound montage begins to build up, Carol's voice mixing with the sounds of the car, night sounds, etc. Julie drops the cleaver and covers her ears, trying to block the sounds out

Mist swirls around Julie

In Julie's mind she is back on the country lane reliving the accident

Sue Please ... Please ...
Julie (*looking down at Sue as though seeing her for the first time*) Carol ...? Oh, my God, Carol! (*She kneels and cradles Sue in her arms; crying*) Oh, Carol ... (*She gently rocks Sue back and forth*) My baby ... My baby ... (*She kisses Sue's head*) It's all right, it's all right, Mummy's here ... (*She looks around desperately*) Help me! Please, somebody help me!

The montage of sound grows. Carol's voice is mixed with the crackle of police-car radios, sirens, snatches of Liz's voice, "Christ, we've hit somebody... then we saw her... Oh, God, there was so much blood...". Throughout this, the sound of the approaching car grows louder and louder

A flashing blue light from a police car can be seen through the windows

Help me! Oh, my God, please help me!

The sound of the car reaches almost deafening proportions. Its headlights appear through the mist

The car rockets towards Julie and Sue, its tyres screeching

Julie (*screaming*) Carol!

The car ploughs into them and there is a sickening thud

There is a simultaneous Black-out and silence

Alternative Ending

Julie Help me! Oh, my God, please help me!

The sound of the approaching car reaches almost deafening proportions. The car brakes and skids with a screech of tyres

  (*Screaming*) Carol!

We hear the sickening thud of the car hitting Carol

There is a simultaneous Black-out and silence

FURNITURE AND PROPERTY LIST

ACT I
SCENE 1

On stage: Ornate 1950s' juke-box
Tapestry
Sofa
Rocking chair
Drinks cabinet with drinks, glasses, a knife
Desk. *On it*: lap-top computer, papers. *Behind it*: junction box, loudspeaker (wired to offstage cassette player, see p. 31)
Telephone
Decorative china plate
Wall safe
Coffee table. *On it*: two glasses
TV and video
Occasional tables
Various speakers (see pp. 30-38)
Fishing twine attached to bookshelf and rocking chair (see p. 30)
Foot switch under rug

Off stage: Gun, torch (**Mike**)
Torch (**Mike**)
Cup of coffee (**Mike**)
Handbag containing small pill bottle and hip flask (**Liz**)

SCENE 2

See text pp. 18-20

SCENE 3

Re-set: Upturned chairs
Drawers pulled out
Books and papers strewn about
Curtains closed, with narrow gap

Set: Clothes, including dressing-gown, on stairs and banisters
Blood on juke-box and surrounding wall, with large smear coming from behind tapestry. *Behind tapestry*: "Carol Mitchell" written in blood, crumpled white dress stained with blood and mud nailed to wall

ACT II
Scene 1

Reset: All furniture to original places
                Piles of books neatly stacked by bookcase

Strike: Clothes, debris

Set: Hammer on cord on outside french windows
                Sports bag on sofa

Off stage: Cassette player (practical; plugged in and wired to onstage
                    loudspeaker and junction box) (**Mike**)
                Mug of coffee (**Julie**)
                Carrier bag (**Sue**)
                Woman's jacket (**Sue**)
                Champagne cork (**Stage Management**)
                Open bottle of champagne, two glasses (**Julie**)

Personal: **Mike**: J-cloth
                Julie: pager

Scene 2

On stage: Curtains and shutters open

Off stage: Trays. *On it*: coffee pot, cream jug, sugar bowl, two cups and saucers
                Wad of cotton wool, medical case (**Julie**)

Scene 3

Set: Dustsheet for **Julie**

Offstage: Cleaver (**Liz**)
                Mobile phone, practical cassette player (with tape of dialogue, see pp.
                    54-55), bag containing roll of carpet tape, clock, **Mike**'s gun (**Julie**)

Personal: **Julie**: gloves

LIGHTING PLOT

Practical fittings required: domestic spotlights, table lamps, light panels on juke-box
Interior with exterior window backing to french windows and landing window,
offstage lights in (unseen) kitchen, porch and bedroom. The same throughout

ACT I, SCENE 1

To open:	Moonlight on exterior backing and through window; juke-box light on	
Cue 1	When ready *House lights down*	(Page 1)
Cue 2	Door opens at head of stairs *Bring up light behind door to shine on to landing*	(Page 1)
Cue 3	**Mike** switches on table lamp by sofa *Snap on table lamp*	(Page 3)
Cue 4	Sound of car driving up *Effect of headlights sweeping past the window*	(Page 4)
Cue 5	**Mike** puts the gun in the wall safe *Snap on light in porch*	(Page 5)
Cue 6	**Mike** switches on the main lights Snap on main lights	(Page 5)
Cue 7	**Mike** switches off the lounge lights *Snap off main lights*	(Page 18)
Cue 8	**Mike** and **Liz** exit into the porch *Snap off porch lights*	(Page 18)
Cue 9	Telephone rings *Fade juke-box light and moonlight*	(Page 18)

ACT I, SCENE 2

See pp. 18-20

Lighting Plot

ACT I, Scene 3

To open:	No interior lights. Moonlight on exterior backing and through windows. Juke-box light on	
Cue 10	**Mike** switches on the wall lights *Snap on wall lights — subdued*	(Page 20)
Cue 11	**Liz** switches off the juke-box *Snap off juke-box light*	(Page 20)
Cue 12	**Mike** switches on alcove spotlights *Snap on alcove spotlights*	(Page 22)
Cue 13	**Mike** switches off all lights *Snap off lights in time with* **Mike**	(Page 25)
Cue 14	**Liz** switches on main room lights *Snap on main room lights*	(Page 26)
Cue 15	**Liz** switches main room lights off *Snap off main room lights*	(Page 26)
Cue 16	**Liz** turns the main room lights back on and switches the alcove spotlights off *Snap on main room lights; snap off alcove lights*	(Page 26)
Cue 17	**Mike**: "Carol Mitchell ... " *Snap off all lights except moonlight*	(Page 27)
Cue 18	**Liz** scrambles to her knees *Snap on kitchen light*	(Page 28)
Cue 19	**Liz**: "Who are you?" *Bring up alcove spotlight slowly*	(Page 29)
Cue 20	**"Carol"**'s voice gets steadily louder *Snap on juke-box light*	(Page 29)
Cue 21	**Liz** falls to the floor *All lights snap to black-out*	(Page 29)

ACT II, Scene 1

To open: Darkness

Cue 22   When ready   (Page 30)
              Bring up half-light effect with shaft of sunlight streaming
              in from landing window; sunlight effect on french window
              backing and through curtains

Cue 23   **Sue**: "I'm right, aren't I?"   (Page 36)
              Snap on juke-box; snap off when **Mike** *switches it off*

Cue 24   **Julie** watches **Mike** go up the stairs   (Page 42)
              Fade lights to black-out

ACT II, Scene 2

To open: Afternoon light effect

Cue 25   **Julie** strokes **Sue**'s cheek   (Page 47)
              Fade lights to black-out

ACT II, Scene 3

To open: Darkness

Cue 26   When ready   (Page 47)
              Bring up moonlight effect on exterior backing
              and through curtains

Cue 27   After a long pause   (Page 47)
              Snap on light behind door to spill on to landing

Cue 28   **Mike** switches on small table tamp   (Page 47)
              Snap on table lamp

Cue 29   **Sue**'s and **Carol**'s voices mingle   (Page 57)
              Fade lights slowly except spot on **Sue**

Cue 30   Montage of sound grows; sound of car gets louder   (Page 58)
              Bring up flashing blue light through windows

Cue 31   Sound of car reaches almost deafening proportions   (Page 58)
              Bring up car headlights through windows, moving
              towards **Julie** *and* **Sue**

| *Cue* 32 | Headlights get to their closest possible; sickening thud *Instant black-out* | (Page 58) |

Alternative Ending

| *Cue* 31 (b) | **Julie**: "Carol!" Sickening thud *Black-out* | (Page 59) |

EFFECTS PLOT

ACT I

Cue 1 As house lights go down   (Page 1)
Sudden loud music chord

Cue 2 **Sue** lets her dress drop to the floor   (Page 2)
Phone rings

Cue 3 **Mike**: "Hallo, the Masons' residence." (Page 3)
Julie's *dialogue over offstage speakers; see script pp. 3-4*

Cue 4 **Julie**: "It's probably just my imagination ——" (Page 4)
Sound of car driving up

Cue 5 **Liz**: "Oh yes. Idiot cards."   (Page 7)
Phone rings

Cue 6 **Liz**: "Hallo ... ? Hallo ... ?"   (Page 7)
Sound of phone being hung up; dialling tone

Cue 7 **Liz** takes pills   (Page 14)
Phone rings

Cue 8 **Liz**: "Hallo, the Masons' residence." (Page 14)
Breathing over offstage speakers

Cue 9 **Liz**: "Look, this is getting beyond a joke." (Page 15)
"Carol"'s *sobbing and dialogue over offstage speakers;
 see script p. 15*

Cue 10 Front door closes   (Page 18)
Sounds of car doors slamming, car driving off; phone rings

NB. ACT I Scene 2 effects: see pp. 18-20

Cue 11 When Scene 3 begins   (Page 20)
"Oh, Carol" plays over juke-box

Cue 12 **Liz** switches the juke-box off   (Page 20)
Cut juke-box sound

Effects Plot

Cue 13	**Liz**: "Nothing seems to have been taken." *Policewoman's dialogue over offstage speakers;* *see script pp.21-22*	(Page 21)
Cue 14	**Liz**: "Oh, God!" *Phone rings*	(Page 28)
Cue 15	**Liz**: "They're trying to get in." *"Carol"'s dialogue over offstage speakers;* *see script pp. 28-29. Sound gradually diffuses* *through onstage speakers, getting louder*	(Page 28)
Cue 16	**"Carol"**'s voice gets steadily louder *Bring up "Oh, Carol" on juke-box; record sticks* *on "I will surely die"; see p 29*	(Page 29)
Cue 17	Rocking chair rocks; books spill from bookcases *Mist seeps from landing and down stairs*	(Page 29)
Cue 18	**Liz** falls to the floor *Juke-box sound snaps off*	(Page 29)

ACT II

Cue 19	**Mike** inadvertently switches the cassette on *"Carol"'s voice over onstage speakers; continue* *until **Mike** switches it off*	(Page 30)
Cue 20	**Sue**: "I'm right, aren't I?" *Juke-box starts to play "Oh, Carol"; continue* *until **Mike** switches it off*	(Page 36)
Cue 21	**Julie**: " ... it's not worth worrying about." *Pager bleeps*	(Page 39)
Cue 22	**Julie** dials the phone *"**Nurse**"'s dialogue over offstage speakers* *(**Liz**'s voice, disguised); see p. 39*	(Page 39)
Cue 23	**Julie**: " ... no one'll look any further." *Phone rings*	(Page 40)
Cue 24	**Mike** (into the phone): "Hallo." *"**Nurse**"'s dialogue over offstage speakers* *(**Liz**'s voice, disguised); see pp. 40-41*	(Page 40)

Cue 40	**Julie**: "Oh, my God, please help me!" *Sound of car reaches almost deafening proportions*	(Page 58)
Cue 41	Car lights rocket towards **Julie** and **Sue** *Screech of tyres*	(Page 58)
Cue 42	Car ploughs into them *Sickening thud*	(Page 58)
Cue 43	Black-out *All sounds cut*	(Page 58)

Alternative Ending

Cue 40(b)	**Julie**: "Oh, my God, please help me!" *Sound of car reaches almost deafening proportions;* *screech of tyres*	(Page 59)
Cue 41(b)	**Julie**: "Carol!" *Sickening thud*	(Page 59)
Cue 42(b)	Black-out *All sounds cut*	(Page 59)

GLOSSARY

The following glossary of English and American expressions can be used to convert **BLOOD MONEY**'s English setting into an American one.

Page	English	American
	ACT I	
	Scene 1	
5	jumper	sweater
6	Television Personality of the Year Award	Daytime Emmy for Outstanding Game Show Host
	Armitage Shanks	Charmin
7	Open University	Meet the Press
9	eighteen	twenty-one
10	sort out your drink problem	straighten out your drinking problem
	smashed	trashed
	dear	love
12	prestigious award	Daytime Emmy
	British public	American public
13	Cochranes	Santinis
	some grotty bedsit above a newsagent's	a roach-infested fifth-floor walk-up
15	heartily	really
16	to London to try and finally win an award	to New York to try and finally win that Emmy
17	crossed line	wrong number
18	that marvellous	all that great

SCENE 2

19	"Television Personality of the Year"	"Daytime Emmy Awards"
	Nancy Edwards	Nancy Glass
	"Television Personality of the Year"	"Outstanding Game Show Host"
	LWT	NBC
	Channel Four	CBS
	Meridian	CBS
	BBC	ABC
	And the winner is ...	And the Emmy for "Outstanding Game Show Host" goes to ...
20	"Television Personality of the Year"	the nation's "Outstanding Game Show Host"

SCENE 3

	test card's	test pattern's
	broken into ...	burglarized
21	mentality'd	sicko would
22	Burgess Hill Police Station	New Hope Police Station
	Rotten luck about the award	Bad luck about the Emmy
	I must say	I gotta tell you
	I'll get on to it right away	I'll get right on it
26	awards	Emmys

ACT II
SCENE 1

31	I'm in a bit of a state	I'm a bit out of it
	popped over	stopped by
	Awards	Emmys
32	how she's getting on	how she's doing
33	Don't be daft	Don't be silly
	Bye for now	*Ciao*

34	come round state her heart was in	regain consciousness condition her heart was in
36	Bacon and eggs	Ham and eggs
37	piss off, Sue	get lost
38	it's all got out of hand You're joking	it's gotten out of hand Are you kidding?
39	No snags?	No complications?

Scene 2

46	surname Hardly	last name Are you kidding?

Scene 3

53	Burgess Hill	New Hope
56	shopping centres BAFTA Westmeston A23 at Pyecombe	malls Emmy New Hope turnpike at exit 17

PRINTED IN GREAT BRITAIN BY
THE LONGDUNN PRESS LTD., BRISTOL.